CONFESSIONS OF AN *IYESKA*

CONFESSIONS OF AN *IYESKA*

Viola Burnette

THE UNIVERSITY OF UTAH PRESS
Salt Lake City

The Defiance House Man colophon is a registered trademark of The University of Utah Press. It is based on a four-foot-tall Ancient Puebloan pictograph (late PIII) near Glen Canyon, Utah.

Library of Congress Cataloging-in-Publication Data

Names: Burnette, Viola, 1938–2016 author.
Title: Confessions of an Iyeska/by Viola Burnette.
Description: Salt Lake City : The University of Utah Press, [2018]
Identifiers: LCCN 2018008704 (print) | LCCN 2018010960 (ebook) |
    ISBN 9781607816409 () | ISBN 9781607816393 (pbk.)
Subjects: LCSH: Burnette, Viola, 1938–2016 | Lakota Indians—Mixed descent—United
    States—Biography. | Lakota women—United States—Biography. | Women lawyers—
    United States—Biography. | Indian judges—United States—Biography. | Indian
    women activists—United States—Biography.
Classification: LCC E99.T34 (ebook) | LCC E99.T34 B88 2018 (print) |
    DDC 978.004/9752440092 [B]—dc23
LC record available at https://lccn.loc.gov/2018008704

While this is a work of nonfiction, some names and details have been changed.

Printed and bound by in the United States of America.

TABLE OF CONTENTS

LIST OF FIGURES

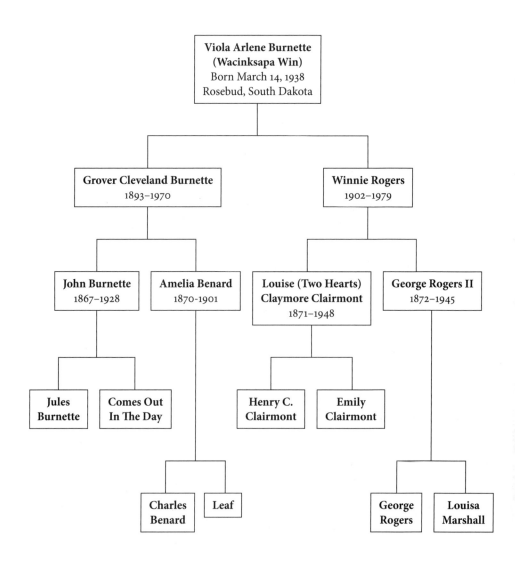

Viola Arlene Burnette
(Wacinksapa Win)
Born March 14, 1938
Rosebud, South Dakota

Grover Cleveland Burnette
1893–1970

Winnie Rogers
1902–1979

John Burnette
1867–1928

Amelia Benard
1870-1901

Louise (Two Hearts)
Claymore Clairmont
1871–1948

George Rogers II
1872–1945

Jules
Burnette

Comes Out
In The Day

Henry C.
Clairmont

Emily
Clairmont

Charles
Benard

Leaf

George
Rogers

Louisa
Marshall

FOREWORD
by Jo Overton

This is the story of our mother, Wacinksapa Win (She Who Seeks Wisdom and Brings it Back), her autobiography. *Confessions of an* Iyeska[1] is the work of many years and hours of our mother's life; she was still working on it the day she died. The only credit my sisters and I deserve is for our constant urging over the years, begging our mother to write down the extraordinary events of her life.

Viola Burnette's life story is inextricably braided together with the history of the Sioux (Lakota) people. She never thought her story was anything special; however, we knew once our mother was gone, not just her story would vanish, but important accounts of the history of our people and our family would be buried with her.

You would not be alone if you thought Indians and treaties were an endnote in the history of the United States. Few people will have more than a passing association with a Native American in their lifetime—existing as part of the past in movies, and usually as the bad guys in books about the westward expansion of America. Natives are depicted as wearing long, feathered headdresses, riding horses, and living in *t'ípis*; the most familiar character portrayed on the big screen is the Sioux warrior. It is forgivable for you to think the people riding the plains, killing innocent pioneers, and hunting for their food have vanished like the huge herds of buffalo that were once part of the landscape: a historical relic, not quite forgotten, but certainly no longer relevant to the twenty-first century.

Many things that happened in the fairly distant past continue to define and impact our present. Few Americans are familiar with the Webster–Ashburton Treaty, but most citizens are aware of the border separating Canada and the United States. It would be unusual to find residents of either community declaring the treaty to be too old, or no longer relevant. Along with the treaty between Britain and the United States, the treaties signed with tribes living across North America continue to be part of both our past and present.

This book will give you an understanding of why it is important for all of us to become more informed about history from a Native standpoint. There is a dismal lack of Native American authors, and when considering female Native authors, the scarcity is appalling. Viola Burnette has created a singular work, bringing together a law degree, history, personal experience, and a woman's perspective into a profoundly moving narrative. Every reader will enter into an intelligent and intimate conversation with the author and leave the final page enlightened.

Some may already know about the problems in Indian country: a high school dropout rate over 50 percent, and a lack of college graduates; crushing poverty with high unemployment; health issues, including endemic tuberculosis and diabetes; and mortality rates of both adults and infants reflecting third-world numbers, not that of an industrialized country. Acquiring an understanding of the generational trauma gives an expanded perspective to some of the underlying problems.

These issues are rooted not just in the past, but from ongoing practices grounded in systematic, racial prejudices. In Viola's lifetime, 1938–2016, there were many instances of widespread discrimination. She was forced by law to attend boarding school, as most Native children were. The primary goal of the boarding schools was annihilation of the Native culture, not the education of the children. Up until the 1960s, many Indians were denied the right to vote by individual states. Even today, discrimination continues to occur at the voting booths, where unreasonable demands by the poll workers deny suffrage to the Native people.

The other side of this story has numerous positive elements. Resilience, determination, generosity, respect for the culture, and a love of laughter are just some of the strengths presented on these pages. Our mother's book will imbue the readers with a sense of awe and respect for her perseverance and strength—her sheer will, to get up again, after you have been knocked down numerous times. Along with historical information, I have no doubt the people who read Viola's book will receive intellectual and emotional gifts. Native or not, this book is for every person. I am Jo, second of my mother's four daughters; my minor part in this story starts in Chapter 8.

PROLOGUE

There was no moon and the night was very dark. Looking out the window through the bars of the metal crib, I could barely see the flicker of lamplight from the windows of our house and the other houses that lined the creek. I had cried all day. I was in the hospital and all alone.

I was three years old, scared and very lonely. My eyes were red and swollen from the hours of crying. In the aftermath, sobs regularly jerked my body. With every ounce of my being, I wished I were out of the hospital and home with Mom, Dad, and my brothers and sisters. In my imagination, I could see Mom getting ready for supper. I could almost hear the laughter of all the neighborhood kids in the last minutes of play before being called in for supper. I remembered the joy of playing hide-and-seek in the near dark. Hiding behind trees and bushes was more fun because it was harder to find everybody in the dark.

Sometimes, whoever was "it" would yell, "olly olly oxen free," when they couldn't find anybody and didn't want to look any longer.

That meant everyone still in hiding could come out without being tagged. Now, I could only imagine the fun. I was really alone.

Earlier that day, I had been overjoyed when Mom came to visit. Seeing her come in the door, I jumped up and down in the crib until the nurse yelled at me to stop. My brother Gibby and I were together in the children's ward, but I missed my mom. Disappointment set in when she said, "I can't stay very long. I have to get over to the store. I came to get Gibby."

I watched with tears in my eyes when the nurse brought Gibby's clothes and helped him dress.

"Momma, take me too," I cried.

"I'm sorry," Momma said. "You're not well, yet. You'll be coming home soon. Don't cry."

I watched them walk out the door. Gibby turned, looked at me, looked at Momma with a question on his face, and then waved to me. I could feel the lump filling my throat and aching. It became unbearable and I threw myself face down on the bed, trying to muffle the sobs, and cried my heart out. I was alone! The fear and loneliness of being in the hospital overwhelmed me.

I was still crying intermittently when the nurse came and began to fuss with the wheels of my crib. I watched curiously, my tears suspended for a moment, as she did something to all four wheels. Suddenly, I was moving. She pushed me through the screen door of the children's ward. Hey, it was fun! I didn't know where I was going, but the ride was fun! She pushed my crib into a small room across the hall. There were two other cribs in the room, but they were empty. She locked the wheels of my crib and left.

I looked around the empty room and my heart sank. The only good thing was that if I stood up I could see over the sill of the only window in the room. I felt a thrill of happiness as I looked out the window. Far, far away, I thought I could see our little house! If I looked hard enough, would I be able to see Momma outside? Or maybe I'd see Gibby outside, playing with the neighbor kids. I strained my eyes, but I wasn't sure which house was ours. I couldn't stop searching with my eyes, and I stood at the window until I was too tired to stand.

Soon after, I realized that I had to use the bathroom. I looked around and there were no other doors in the room to indicate that there was a bathroom near. The legs of the crib were about three feet high and the sides of the iron-barred crib were formidable. It seemed impossible for me to climb out and hit the floor safely. Worst of all, I'd be in trouble! The nurse would yell, and she might even hit me!

I sat in my crib. Alone and miserable, my bladder began to ache. I watched the hallway, hoping for a nurse to pass by.
I heard rapid footsteps and cried out, "Nurse!"

But, it wasn't audible. My fear kept my voice still. I waited longer, trying to gather my courage. I had to call the nurse or I'd be in bigger trouble when I wet my bed! I began to cry again and eventually I cried myself to sleep. Sometime in the night, I wakened to hear a nurse walking by and called to her without thinking. She took me across the hall to the bathroom in the children's ward and then back to that little room.

The next morning, in the early hours, I was awakened by a nurse swabbing my left hip with something cold. Startled, I watched her pick up what appeared to be a huge syringe and stab me in the hip with it. Then, I was alone again. It happened so fast I didn't have time to get scared.

I don't remember why I was in the hospital. The memory of that "shot" still haunts me. The incident was burned into my child's memory by the trauma of my mother and brother leaving me alone and by the added loneliness of that little room. Eventually, I developed a huge "boil" on my hip that had to be treated with ointments and bandages and it was very sore. I remained alone in that little room, isolated from the other kids in the children's ward until my discharge. There has always been a question in my mind about why I was isolated and why I was given that shot. It may have been a smallpox vaccination. When I was older I asked Mom why I was given a shot in my hip and she didn't know. She never asked.

Years later, I was at boarding school and had to have an operation. I was taken to the hospital, operated on, and returned to school, all without my parents ever knowing that anything had happened. It was as if they didn't have a right to know. My parents never questioned the right of the doctors and nurses to do whatever they chose. It was assumed that they knew what was right for us and that they wouldn't hurt us.

Although I was unaware of it, this small episode was a classic example of the influences that shaped the lives of Lakota people. My parents were part of the third generation of Lakota people who were forced out of the old way of life. T'ípis gone along with the ability to provide for themselves, they had to depend on the government for their livelihood. Under such circumstances, it was inevitable that the government would use the power of deprivation to control and oppress the people. Food and housing were at a premium. Anyone who sought help in getting even the basics of life had to bow to the wishes of government officials. The US Army was in charge and they were typically authoritarian and cruel. It wasn't uncommon for them to withhold rations to enforce an order or change an unwanted behavior. Along with withholding the necessities of life came the practice of belittling the people, calling them dirty, lazy, and other denigrating slurs designed to undermine their pride and self-reliance. The oppression has resulted in a population that is atypical in its reaction to authority.

By the time my mother took me to the hospital, wanting good care for me and my brother, she had been regulated and disciplined from birth. She had no choice and dared not question the caregivers.

Author, Viola Burnette, age three (ca. 1941), in Rosebud, South Dakota.

One

LAKOTA BEGINNINGS

In order to understand the ups and downs of my life, you need to know a bit about history—American Indian history, which is somewhat different than what you may have learned in school. That history includes the lives of my parents and grandparents. By the time I was born, my tribe, the Brulé Sioux people, had barely begun the process of adjusting to living on the reservation. I was part of the third generation of Indians to do so. Our people had to go from living in freedom and independence to a life of restriction and reliance on other people. We are still adjusting.

All of my great-grandmothers were born sometime around 1850. During that time, the Brulé Sioux people were well settled into life in what became known as Dakota Territory. Their primary concern was survival. They took care of their families the natural way, hunting and gathering their food and fighting off the enemies who would endanger their lives.

In 1851, the first legal intrusion from the United States government occurred to interfere in their everyday lives. The Fort Laramie Treaty of 1851 sought to reduce the land base the Lakota used for hunting and to impose territorial boundaries upon the tribes who lived and hunted in the area of the Oregon Trail and the prospective transcontinental railway.[1] The United States wanted peaceful tribes so their people could travel safely through Dakota Territory. They asked the Sioux to follow the boundaries set out in the treaty and to stop fighting the other tribes over hunting territory. For such peace, they said they were willing to pay to the Indians provisions, merchandise, animals, and so on.

What this meant to my great-great-grandparents was that they were told that they were no longer free to simply follow the buffalo or other game. The white man's peace wasn't always possible, especially as they began to rely on the provisions they were promised that were not forthcoming. Boundaries on paper meant nothing, and the tribes continued to live as they always had. White people, however, believed the treaty meant they could go wherever they wanted, and they began to appear in greater numbers.

In the 1860s, in response to the continuing strife between the tribes and the demands of white people for more land, the US government set about making treaties with the tribes—assuring them that they would be able to live unmolested on land of their own and that they would be provided with rations to make up for their inability to hunt as they always had.

The 1868 Treaty of Fort Laramie with the Sioux and the Agreement with the Sioux of 1867 changed the world of Sioux people.[2,3] The treaty set out the boundaries of what would become known as the Great Sioux Reservation. The Lakota people were, once again, promised that the land set aside for them would be theirs alone, although specific sections of the reservation were set aside as smaller reservations for particular tribes. The land also included land set aside for hunting grounds and the Black Hills.

The *He Sápa* (Black Hills) are and always have been sacred ground to the Lakota people. It's a place to go for contemplation and prayer. It was named the Black Hills because, from a distance, the stands of pine trees make the hills appear to be black.

There had been rumors of gold in the Black Hills for many years. In 1876, the US government sent surveyors, engineers, and other scientists to explore the Black Hills to determine whether or not the rumors were true. When it was discovered that gold truly existed in the Black Hills, a gold rush began.

In order to overcome the heated objections of the Sioux warriors and to protect all of the white settlers and gold seekers, Congress passed the Agreement with the Sioux of 1876 in which they rescinded the section of the Treaty of 1868 giving the Lakota absolute right to the Black Hills. They wanted to pay for the land with subsistence rations. The treaty required that, in order to change the land provisions, two-thirds of the Lakota men had to agree to sign. All but 10 percent refused and a war ensued.

Congress still won. They passed the Indian Appropriations Act of 1876,[4] which cut off all rations for the Sioux until they terminated hostilities and ceded the Black Hills to the United States. It was aptly named the "sign or die" amendment.

Gradually, the Sioux chiefs realized that their defeat was complete and in order to save their people they would have to succumb to the demands of the US government. Those demands resulted in each leader taking his people to live on the designated reservations. The Black Hills were lost but not forgotten.

It would take one hundred years and a lawsuit against the United States government for the Lakota people to find a small measure of justice. The United States Supreme Court found that the US government had taken the land in the Black Hills without compensating the Lakota people. They ordered that the government pay $106 million in compensation. It was not what they wanted. They wanted their land back. To this day when the people gather, you will hear the cry, "the Black Hills are not for sale."

With the continuing influx of white settlers, gold seekers, and the overpowering army, Chief Spotted Tail and others were forced to sign the treaty to protect their families from annihilation. The treaty included an agreement that their land base would be further reduced. The terms of surrender were clear: give up your guns, become peaceable, and we will take care of you. They signed the treaty and gave up their land, their freedom, and their independence.

By the fall of 1868, the Brulé and Oglala Sioux had been moved to Whetstone Agency on the Missouri River and my great-grandmothers went with them.[5] All four of my great-grandmothers grew up in the typical Lakota way of life, following the buffalo and learning to live in unity with their environment. By the time they were old enough to marry, there were increasing numbers of white men who wanted to be part of their world. White trappers and traders were looking for wives who could survive the hardships of prairie life. My great-grandmothers, Louisa, Emily, *Waȟpé* (Leaf), and Comes-Out-In-The-Day, were perfect and the time was right. They were looking for security in a changing world as were the men they married.

My father's father, John Burnette, was born somewhere around Fort Laramie, Wyoming, about the time the Treaty of 1868 was signed. John's

Jules Burnette, circa 1867, Fort Laramie, Wyoming.

mother, Comes-Out-In-The-Day (later renamed Mary), was there with
Chief Spotted Tail's band and Chief Spotted Tail was there to sign the
treaty. In my imagination, I picture Comes-Out-In-The-Day, perhaps
sitting on the ground, taking part in the negotiations over the treaty.
Maybe she didn't get to share her opinion as the men of her band did,
but I'm certain she voiced those opinions around her own campfire.

Born in Canada, Juel (or Jules) Burnette was a trapper for the American Fur Company. Mom's story about them was that Jules needed a wife
and asked around the camp for a good woman. Everyone spoke highly of
Comes-Out-In-The-Day and he decided to marry her. She was a beautiful
young woman, but she spoke no English when she met Jules Burnette.

In November 1867, Jules, along with several other men, signed a
petition to Congress asking for land so they could support their Lakota
families. The petition was never granted; sometime after John's birth,
Jules went into the Snowy Mountains in Wyoming to do some trapping
and never came back.

By the winter of 1868, the people were showing the deprivation
brought on by months of dependence on the US government. Their clothes
were ragged and *t'ípi* covers were falling apart.[6] Worst of all, rations were
either slow or absent. They couldn't hunt, and it cost them dearly.

Comes-Out-In-The-Day, circa 1867, Fort Laramie, Wyoming.

Recently, my daughter Jan and I took a road trip to reflect on the experience of my great-grandmothers at the Whetstone Agency. Using what little information we had, we drove down the main highway, watching for the sign and then down country roads to find our way to the banks of the Missouri River. At the end of the road there was a small park for tourists. We parked next to the only other car present and got out of the car. We should have driven farther north to the White River, but our time was limited. We were in Whetstone Township, where the Lakota had once lived free and hunted. I knew we were walking in their footsteps.

We stood on the banks of the "Mighty Mo" and I searched my soul for generational memories of my *uŋcici* (great-grandmother). The cold wind blew off the water and whipped up tiny waves on the surface. The river was dark blue-gray, reflecting the sky that was gray with rain clouds. It touched my heart and brought out the sadness I knew must have permeated the lives of the Lakota people as they tried to make sense of their new life. They had been here before, but this time they didn't have the resources necessary to sustain their families. A mother's heart would break when her child cried from hunger. Warriors would agonize over their inability to provide for their families. As I sat on the edge of the river, I said a *wopila* (thank-you prayer) to my ancestors for their sacrifices that I might live.

All that's left now is a state recreation area called Whetstone Recreation Area and the mournful ghosts of buckskin-clad prisoners of war.

The Whetstone Agency was meant to be a gathering place for the Sioux tribes prior to being dispersed to various reservations. It wasn't that simple; some tribes wanted to choose their own living places. Chief Spotted Tail hated Whetstone because of its proximity to the Missouri River, giving his people free access to alcohol. Red Cloud, chief of the Oglala, didn't like Whetstone either.

Nevertheless, Whetstone became the birthplace for two of my grandparents in the 1870s. *Wahpé* married Charles Benard and they gave birth to my grandmother, Amelia, as well as two other daughters. It was obvious that *Wahpé* would Christianize her children since she had been baptized in the Episcopal Church. She, along with many other Lakota women, chose to marry white men and to learn how to live in the white world.

Emily, whose Indian name is lost, and who was a sister to Chief Ring Thunder, married a white trader, Henry Claymore or Clairmont, and gave birth to my maternal grandmother, Two Hearts (Louise) in 1871. In 1872, my grandfather, George II, was born to Louisa Marshall and George Rogers, who was a freighter. Louisa's mother was an Oglala, the daughter of Chief Little Wound, and they were probably living among Chief Red Cloud's band at this time.

Chief Spotted Tail's band would move several times in the next few years. He never liked Whetstone because shipping on the Missouri River made liquor available to the people, and he was aware of the damage it was wreaking on them.[7] It wasn't until 1878 that they finally settled in Rosebud.[8]

At the same time, Chief Red Cloud's band settled in Pine Ridge. The Lakota people settled into what would become the state of South Dakota.

In 1887, the passage of the Dawes Act began to shatter the land holdings of the Lakota people.[9] The promised "land of our own" would be chipped away by legal finagling. The Dawes Act had been passed in 1887 to break up the reservations formed in 1851 and 1868 by the Fort Laramie treaties and, ostensibly, to provide individuals with their own land. All Indian households were allotted 160 acres of land and single members received 80 acres. Did it matter that the land "given" wasn't enough to provide a living for anyone? No, it didn't matter because after each Indian was given their allotment of land, lo and behold, there was enough land "left over" to provide thousands of white settlers with their own land. The land grab that had begun with the Fort Laramie Treaty of 1851 continued.

The 1889 Agreement with the Sioux followed, to finish the breakup of the Great Sioux Reservation.[10] It established smaller land bases for each of the Sioux Reservations and excluded many, many acres, which left the land free to be offered to settlers. Heartbreak for Lakota people was bounty for others.

As for my own family, Comes-Out-In-The-Day, accepting the loss of Jules Burnette, took baby John and went with the rest of Chief Spotted Tail's band as they were moved farther east. There she met Adam Smith, who had settled in what would become Mellette County, South Dakota. They married, or maybe they just moved in together, which was common in an area that lacked churches and ministers.

Adam was known as a good man. He taught John everything he knew about ranching and business. Because of Adam, John and Mary would never know the hardships of living reservation life under the control of the federal government.

Most of the Lakota people were entirely dependent on the army to provide for their daily needs. According to the story told to my mother, her family would travel by horse and wagon to the agency to collect the rations they needed. She told me about the crowds that gathered at the agency offices, traveling for miles. They brought their tents and camped to await the arrival of much-needed rations.

Wagonloads of meat would be brought in along with staples such as sugar, flour, and coffee. In the beginning, the beef was delivered on the hoof. The people butchered the cattle just as they had the buffalo. Then the government began to deliver the meat already cut up.

Here, my soft-spoken mother's voice took on an edge as she passed on her sad history. I could tell that her childhood memories still bothered her.

More often than not, the cut-up meat was rotten or didn't arrive at all and people went hungry. So much for treaty obligations! My grandparents had to learn to survive and adjust to the white man's world.

When he was twenty years old, John became eligible to receive his own allotment of land under the Dawes Act. Until then, John had been known as John Smith.

As he went to apply for the land, his stepfather, Adam, told him, "You had better use your real name, Burnette."

Amelia Benard (right) and friend.

As it turned out, no one was named Smith because even Adam had changed his name. When Comes-Out-In-The-Day died, Adam wrote on her tombstone, "Mary Smith, beloved wife of Adolf Schmidt."

John, half-breed that he was, lived in both worlds. His stepfather helped him assimilate into white society, and he became an adept businessman and rancher. John established a butcher shop in the town of White River in addition to a boarding house/café. He became one of those ranchers who provided cattle to the army to provide meat rations to the *oyate* (people, nation).

John's mother, then known as Mary, nurtured his ties to Lakota culture. She spoke very little English so she spoke Lakota to John. Later on, she passed the language on to my father and his sister, Grace. She believed

John and Amelia Burnette's marriage portrait.

in Lakota spirituality and enriched the lives of her son and grandchildren with traditional stories and songs.

In 1890, John married Amelia Benard, who gave birth to my Aunt Grace in 1891 and my dad in 1893. She had four more children who didn't survive infancy, which was common in those days.

When Dad was eight years old, Amelia gave birth to a son, who they named Jules, after John's father. As was the practice, a midwife was called to attend the birth. There wasn't a doctor available, and the midwife who attended the birth did the best she could. She couldn't stop the bleeding and Amelia knew she was going to die. She made John promise to bury her beside her father, Charles Benard, in Rosebud. She was thirty years old. There is no gravesite for Amelia's mother, *Waȟpé*, and I would assume that, since she was a full-blood, she must have been placed in a scaffold rather than buried in the fashion of white men.[11]

Within days of Amelia's death, John took the baby Jules and, by horse and wagon, traveled about eighty or ninety miles to a place called Keya

Grover and Grace Burnette, circa 1898, Mellette County,
South Dakota.

Paha, where Amelia's sister Julia lived with her husband, William Raymond. Julia cared for Jules for three months until, tragically, he too died.
When my Raymond cousins showed me where he was buried, my heart
ached for him and I felt that I had finally met the grandmother I never
knew. She started me on my journey to find out more about my family.

John remarried and had more children, but Grandma Mary continued to be a force in Dad's life. Dad grew up living the life of a cowboy
and prospective businessman but never forgot his Lakota roots.

Adam Smith, Grover Burnette, and John Burnette (left to right), circa 1918, Mellette County, South Dakota.

John Burnette (right) in his butcher shop, circa 1912, White River, South Dakota.

My mother's parents, Two Hearts (Louise) Clairmont and George Rogers, who were both mixed-bloods, were born just prior to the Battle of the Little Big Horn (1876) in which George Armstrong Custer was killed. Even though it is hailed as a victory for us, it was the beginning of the end of a way of life for Indians and my grandparents were caught up in the trauma and turmoil. By the time they married in 1891, Congress had already acted to ensure (they thought) the demise of tribes.

My maternal grandfather, George Jr., was born in 1872 to Louisa Marshall, an Oglala Sioux, and George Rogers, a white freighter. The first George was another one of those people who just disappeared on the prairie, so we don't have any records about him. My mother said he was a freighter, someone who drove a freight wagon pulled by a team of horses. She said her grandfather went on a freighting trip and never came back. Who knows? Maybe he died on the prairie and maybe he found someone more enticing along the way. At any rate, young George was an infant and their only child. Louisa remarried, to a man named Meddore Douville, and had six more children. As an adult, George Jr. joined the army to survive and was stationed at Fort Niobrara, Nebraska.[12]

He and other mixed-bloods like him were sometimes called Indian scouts. Some called them traitors because their predecessors, those who

Louisa Marshall (far left) and sisters.

worked for the army, were thought to be aiding the army to the detriment of their own people.

Even though the time for warfare had passed by the time George joined the army, the stigma must have remained because I remember, as a child, feeling that I wasn't allowed to talk about it. There was a sense that it was shameful to have been an Indian scout. I know little or nothing about Grandpa George's upbringing or his relationship to Lakota culture. I have to think that the transition into the white world couldn't have been easy, and I'm sorry I didn't know him.

Louise Clairmont's mother, Emily Trapan, was sister to Chief Ring Thunder and Louise's upbringing was very traditional even though her father was white.[13] Henri Clairmont was a fur trader who had a store on the Missouri River. My grandmother Louise, exposed to Christian missionary teaching, tried to practice Catholicism at first and then became an Episcopalian. She tried very hard to be a good Christian, but when the going was tough, she always turned to her belief in Lakota spirituality. The *Canupa* (sacred pipe) was her mainstay.[14] George and Louise had seven children between 1895 and 1912. They were divorced sometime

Louise (Two Hearts) Clairmont (third from left), circa 1892.

George Rogers Jr., circa 1893, Fort Niobrara, Nebraska.

after 1912. Gram Louise would marry twice more, but she had no more children.

These four people, my grandparents, were our family's bridge between the old way of life and the future. Being an *Iyeska*[15] (half-breed/ mixed-blood) was never easy. They were admired by some and reviled by others. They traveled a path unexplored and unmarked. Each had to choose that path, and they were not always comfortable with their choices. Their strength and courage would leave us a legacy of pride and endurance.

My father was Grover Burnette, first-born son of John Burnette and Amelia Benard. Tall and burly, he was a hard worker. He briefly attended an Indian boarding school in Rapid City, but he had no other schooling.

He spent his growing up years learning to work as a cowboy and rancher. He spoke fluent English and Lakota and loved to tell stories and jokes. I don't recall that he ever complained about any consequence of being a mixed blood. He was proud of his Lakota upbringing.

My mother, Winnie Rogers, was a good Christian, but she was a good Lakota woman first. Kind, gentle, and soft-spoken, she was also tough and determined. She went to Indian boarding schools, St. Mary's Episcopal Girls' School and Genoa Indian Industrial School. As a result of the indoctrination at school, she became a staunch Christian. She never participated in any Lakota sacred ceremonies and denounced them as heathen, but she continued to take part in cultural practices.

To start with, my life was fairly typical of the lives of American Indian people. I was born on the Rosebud Indian Reservation in the late 1930s. I was the ninth of ten children, and prior to my birth my parents lived in different places. Housing was very short on the reservation, and there were times when my parents lived in a tent. Gone were the days of the buffalo and *t'ípis*, and the tent was army surplus.

When I was born, the family lived in a little white house on the banks of what is now called Squaw Creek, just below the Rosebud Agency offices. Life was difficult on the reservation in the '20s and '30s, and my parents were fortunate to have a house. It had four rooms: a living room, dining room, kitchen, and one bedroom with a walk-in closet. Two of my sisters, Marjorie and Martha, slept in the bedroom while my oldest sister, Eleanor, slept in the closet. She was privileged by her status as the eldest daughter. There would have been another sister, but she was stillborn in 1934. My brothers slept in the dining room on bedrolls, and Mom and Dad had a double bed in the living room. There was no electricity, so we had kerosene lamps for lighting and a wood stove for heat. We didn't have running water either. Mom planted a small garden next to the house to help feed her brood of children. Gardening was new to the Lakota then, so I have to give credit to my mother for being so progressive.

My mother and father always worked. Mom cleaned the Bureau of Indian Affairs agency offices at times. She also worked for Mr. and Mrs. Damm, who owned a grocery store/café. She worked in the store and café as clerk, waitress, and cook. She also cleaned house for the Damms and other people. She was more than an employee to Mr. and Mrs. Damm, who were not Indian. She was their friend and remained

LAKOTA BEGINNINGS | 21

so until their deaths. While she worked, my older sisters cared for the youngest of us. Dad was, at different times, police officer, road maintenance worker, rancher, and tribal judge.

Life in Rosebud may have been difficult, but we were a happy family. Our community was small and close-knit. It was made up of Lakota families and we were all related in one way or another. We children were expected to be obedient and respectful. We all had chores to do around the house, but we had plenty of play time. There were times when some of us quarreled, but we were forbidden to hit one another. True to Lakota tradition, my parents never spanked us.

One day my older sister, Marge, lacking any other form of communication, sent me on a trip down the street to give her best friend a note. She promised me something or other in return for my hurrying back. On the way back, I cut across Mom's garden and had to climb a small fence. For some reason, I was wearing my Sunday shoes, a pair of black Mary Janes. On the way over the fence, one of the buckles on my shoe caught on the fence and was torn off. I was devastated—not because I feared punishment, but because I knew they couldn't be replaced. Marge did her best to sew the buckle back on my shoe, but it would never be the same. In a time when corporal punishment was common in mainstream society, it never occurred to my parents to spank me for tearing up my irreplaceable shoes.

Some of us had nicknames that stuck for a lifetime. My oldest brother, Grover Jr., became "Doc" because he was so serious and wore glasses. Sister Eleanor became "Deed" for unknown reasons, and Marge was nicknamed "Teewee" for the rest of her life. "Teta" was Martha's nickname and only complete strangers ever called her by her given name. My brother Gilbert became "Gib"; John was simply "Johnny"; Robert was "Bob"; and baby Arthur James, named for Mom and Dad's friend, Mr. Damm, was "Jimmy." To my dismay, my nickname, for a time, was "Knobby." It hurt my feelings because it was given to me to make fun of my nose. The name stuck until I discovered that my nose was just like Dad's. Eventually, Mom and Dad decreed that anyone who called me "Knobby" had to pay me a nickel. It didn't take long for the name to disappear.

Since our community was so small and everyone knew everyone else, we children had a lot of freedom. Lakota people lived the axiom "it takes a village to raise a child," and we were always under the watchful eye of every adult in the community.[16] Having been taught respect for our elders, we obeyed all adults. It worked very well for everyone. Parents always knew where their children were and what they were doing. Children always knew they could go to anyone for help if they needed it.

Two

GROWING UP ON THE FARM

In 1934, Congress passed the Indian Reorganization Act (IRA) to encourage tribes to set up their own governments.[1] By referendum vote, the Rosebud Sioux Tribe accepted a prewritten constitution and bylaws. Never having participated in such a process, they had no idea what they were accepting. They even accepted the name, "Rosebud Sioux Tribe." The name was chosen for the wild roses that still grow in the area. It would be many years later before the people realized that their tribal name had been changed without their permission. The *Sicangu Oyate* (people of the burnt thigh) would have great difficulty reclaiming their lost identity.[2] Time and oppression would cement the name "Rosebud Sioux Tribe."

After years of deprivation and poverty, 1936 brought a wave of attempts at economic and social reform for Indian people. The Indian Relief and Rehabilitation Division (IRRD) was formed within the Bureau of Indian Affairs to implement reform at Rosebud. The IRRD set out to rehabilitate approximately twenty Indian communities in South Dakota, including the one called Two Kettle.[3]

Two Kettle became our home in 1942. It was eighteen miles from the town of White River, and we traveled a graveled "highway" until we reached a bridge to cross the Little White River—and there began a dirt road that would lead to our house. Somewhere between the bridge and our house there was a confluence of the Big and Little White Rivers. The Big White cut through the valley, which was surrounded by hills covered with prairie grass and a few trees. Trees lined the banks of the river(s) and provided some stability for sandy-chalky soil that also colored the river water. Swimming, we would come out covered with a layer of white silt. It didn't matter because we only counted the fun.

There were eight families in the valley and a white "Boss Farmer" who was supposed to help everyone transition to farm life. Seven of the families were "given" a certain amount of acreage and a small, two-bedroom log house. In actuality, nothing was given to the families since the land and houses continued to be owned by the tribe. All we got to keep was the profit from our labor.

The families were all learning to farm together, including the wives. Since we had the largest house, it became a gathering place. There were quilting and sewing bees, and I remember the ladies would cut up old discarded woolen coats for quilts. These were favored because they were so warm in winter. Lined with old flannel sheets and filled with cotton batting, only one quilt was needed for each bed. Mom had a treadle sewing machine that was operated by a pedal that was rocked up and down with your foot. I learned to sew on that machine and spent many happy hours sewing with Mom.

We also had Episcopal Church services in our house from time to time. One Sunday, my brothers and I chose to sit out church services upstairs. We watched the services through the heat register. Bending over, chewing on a carrot, little Jim dropped a piece that landed in the lap of an elderly woman. "Oh, my goodness!" she exclaimed, "carrots from heaven." Everyone laughed, but Mom was mortified.

Our house was one of two two-story houses that had been built sometime before we moved there. The story we heard was that it was built by a wealthy banker who was dissatisfied after he built the first house so he built another. There was also a story that they were built for a chief. Neither house had electricity or running water, but the second house had electric wiring and a furnace in the basement. We lived in the first house, and in 1947 my brother Bob married and lived in the second house. The two houses were about 100 yards apart, and the second house was destined to become our school house.

Before we arrived to begin farming, the government had set up the irrigation project. In ravines in the hills above our valley, small reservoirs were dug to hold the runoff from snow and rain. Ditches were dug, sluice gates installed, and we waited for the flow of water to water the crops and

Two Kettle, the Burnette farm, circa 1942.

speed us on the way to success. The water never came. The plan to pump the water from the river wasn't feasible, and the reservoirs could barely water the cattle. The soil in the floor of the valley proved to be clay and not amenable to growing most crops. In fact, after a rain, it turned to "gumbo," a waxy, silty soil that becomes very sticky. It clumped on the wheels of vehicles, horses' hooves, and people's feet and soon made it practically impossible to move.

After several years of trying to grow corn, barley, and wheat for profit, my father decided that alfalfa was the best crop he could grow. He increased his herd of cattle and became rancher rather than farmer. The alfalfa fed our horses and cattle and provided an additional small income when it was sold as feed for livestock. Gradually, the other families in the valley gave up and left. The tiny plots of land they were given were inadequate and they couldn't make a living as farmers. Dad leased the land they had held and soon we were the only ones left.

In addition to the house and land, we also had use of a chicken coop, pigpen, and a huge barn to shelter cows and horses. The barn had a hayloft to store hay, stalls for horses, head stalls to hold the milk cows still

Author's brother John Burnette; father, Grover Burnette Sr.; and friend branding calves.

while they were being milked, and a small calf pen for the milk cows' calves. Attached to the barn, there was a large corral. We also had a windmill that pumped drinking water for the animals and provided us a place to play and a swimming hole for our dog. The water wasn't drinkable, and we had to haul our drinking water from two miles away. We had all the equipment necessary for farming. In the beginning, all the farm equipment was horse-drawn. Eventually, tractors would ease the burden of labor for Dad and my brothers, but it was always hard work.

Dad would often take Jim and me to the fields with him. He would hold one of us on his lap while the other was allowed to ride the horse that was working. He used the time with us to teach us, through stories, about nature and spirituality. One day, we watched a meadowlark land in front of the horse. She walked slowly away from us, dragging one of her wings. Dad said in a low voice, "Watch her. She's trying to get us away from her nest." As soon as we passed by, she flew away, daring us to follow. I remember thinking that my dad knew everything.

Lakota people have a rich tradition of teaching by storytelling. I do remember Dad repeating *Iktómi* stories, but I don't recall the details.[4] *Iktómi* is a mischievous magical spider who teaches lessons through getting into trouble himself and suffering the consequences. I learned about the prairie chicken mating dance through an *Iktómi* story. I'm sorry I can't tell the story. I was really too young to understand the moral of the story, and I just remember being awed by the idea of prairie chickens dancing.

I was four years old and the next couple of years were very happy for me. We had moved into what I thought was a huge house. It had three bedrooms—one for the boys and one for the girls upstairs and one for Mom and Dad downstairs, next to the living room. There was a dining room that was as large as the living room, and the two rooms were separated by an archway. The living room was furnished with an upholstered couch, two matching wicker rocking chairs for Mom and Dad, a square accent table with glass balls for feet that had been given to Mom when she got married, and a pot-bellied stove for heat.

Kerosene lamps and lanterns lit our way at night. During the last milking of the day, it was comforting to watch the cows being milked by the soft light of the lantern and listen to the regular sound of the milk hitting the side of the bucket—ping, ping or splashing, squish, squish—as it filled the bucket. We had barn cats and if the kittens mewed for milk, my brothers would squirt milk directly into their mouths. Sometimes Jim and I would try to practice our rodeo skills by trying to ride the little calves whose mothers were being milked.

Since I was the youngest girl, I was the constant butt of my siblings' teasing. I was afraid of the dark and my sister Teta simply loved to scare me. She told me stories about a wild cat that had lost one eye and would chase little girls. One evening at dusk, when I knew the milking had just begun, I started the short walk to the barn. As I passed the corner of the house, a cat streaked by me, startling me. I screamed and my sister yelled, "One-eyed cat!" Terrified, instead of turning around and running for the house, I ran, crying, straight to the barn where Dad and the boys were milking. Needless to say, everyone thought it was hilarious that I was terrified of a one-eyed cat. The story became one that was repeated on every family occasion.

In the summer, once all the evening chores were done, we'd sit outside and build a smudge fire to keep the mosquitoes away. We'd watch as night fell and bats came flying out of the barn. When they dipped low, we would cover our heads with our arms, afraid they would tangle in our hair.

In winter, we gathered in the living room. By kerosene lamplight, we would read or Dad would tell stories. Oh, and I nearly forgot—we had a radio! It was powered by a car battery. Dad listened to the news at six o'clock without fail and he loved boxing. He would listen to the Friday night fights and always seemed to know who was going to win. We kids were allowed to listen to our favorite programs such as the *Lone Ranger* and *Hopalong Cassidy*. Mom's favorites were *Fibber McGee and Molly* and soap operas like *Guiding Light*.

The radio was small, about a foot high and maybe eighteen inches wide. It sat on a small table next to Dad's rocking chair, with the car battery underneath. It was secondhand but in fairly good shape except for the fact that the tuning knobs were loose and came off easily.

One day, Dad came in to listen to the news. I was in the kitchen with Mom when I heard him roar, "Where is that knob?" He didn't sound happy, and my response was immediate. I went running to the living room, saying, "Here I am, Daddy!" The incident became another family joke, retold every time any of us were together.

The dining room was the hub of our house. It was fully occupied by a very large table, some chairs, and a bench that could seat four kids in a pinch. Many evenings we gathered at the dining room table to play games and cards, eat fudge and popcorn, and to just be together. Penny ante poker was our favorite game, sometimes played with pennies and sometimes with tooth picks. I did so want to learn to "bluff" like Johnny, but it remained a mystery how it was done.

One night we were playing poker, as usual. Johnny was winning and he kept up a steady round of jokes, probably to distract us from thinking too much about what was happening. My brother Bob rarely played with us, but his wife, Bea, enjoyed our company. On this occasion, it was obvious that Bea thought she had a winning hand. She bet heavily, hoping to force Johnny to withdraw. Finally, it was just Johnny and Bea and it was time for a show of hands. They laid down their cards simultaneously.

Suddenly, Dad said in a loud voice, "Dead man's hand!": aces and eights, just like the cards in the hand held by Wild Bill Hickok the day he was killed in Deadwood, South Dakota. His fearsome and very loud voice and the words "dead man" caused Bea to leap out of her chair, knocking it over.

She screamed, "Yaaaaw!"

She threw up her hands and started to cry before she realized she had been pranked. The rest of us, after a moment of startle, laughed until we cried.

There was a window in the middle of the south wall and the table was centered in front of it. Right above the bench, which was next to the wall, Mom had placed a shelf, which always held house plants of varying species. She loved those plants, especially in winter, and we learned to duck our heads when we sat down at the table. There was also a white cupboard with a metal shelf that slid in and out to be used for counter space. Mom's prized possession was a sideboard that had two side doors and two drawers in the middle. There she kept a few nice linens and special dishes.

In the beginning, we had an ice box in the dining room on the north wall. It was made of wood and stood about five feet tall. It had double doors, but no shelves. When we could get it, the bottom portion held a block of ice. Needless to say, it wasn't often that we could get ice for it and we used the cellar steps to store perishables for short periods. In the end, it was relegated to the back porch to store things that had no other place.

Mom saved small amounts from her jobs in town and eventually she bought a propane gas refrigerator and stove. It was no small feat, and we were all thrilled. Mostly, we didn't need to store food. We never had leftovers, and all produce was eaten straight out of the garden.

Eggs and milk were eaten fresh every day. We had a cream separator that separated the cream from the milk. We made our own butter from the cream using a one-gallon churn with wooden paddles. I remember my arms aching with the effort of turning the handle. The skim milk left from the separation was either made into cottage cheese or fed to the pigs. I suppose someone might have drunk it, but I didn't. I hated the taste of it. Extra milk, eggs, or produce were taken to town and sold.

During the summer, Mom had a garden close to the house that was about fifty yards square. There was a constant stream of vegetables being cooked and canned or dried all summer. I loved it when she canned corn. We helped shuck the husks from the corn and saved them for the horses. I loved to chew on the fat end of the husks because they were so sweet. Mom would boil the corn and slice it off the cob. I sat on the floor close by so I could grab the cobs and chew off the sweet nubs of the corn. I still think that's the best part of corn on the cob. The residue of the corn was given to the pigs.

The kitchen of our house was about eight feet square and held a huge, black, cast-iron stove. Fired up at least three times a day, it provided warmth and comfort. It had four removable plates as a cooking surface and a hot-water well on the side. The only other furniture in the room was a small table, covered with a tin top, probably three feet by three feet, used as a work surface. In addition, there was a wash stand that held the water bucket, dipper, and wash basin.

Adjacent to the kitchen was a walk-in pantry that held nonperishable food stuffs: canned goods, baking essentials, twenty-five-pound bags of flour, and a bin for potatoes. The entrance to the cellar was also in the pantry. In the cellar there was a huge bin for potatoes. In the spring we spent a good deal of time cutting the potatoes into small sections, each containing an "eye," to be used as seed for a new crop. Dad built shelves in the basement to hold all the vegetables, fruits, and yes, beef, pork, and chicken, canned by Mom to feed everyone through the next year.

We would go out "hunting" for plums, choke cherries, and buffalo berries for Mom to can. We'd use a horse and wagon since there were no roads where the berries grew. One year, Dad was driving the horses and looking for choke cherry bushes instead of watching where he was going. He didn't see the tree stump that passed between the horses but caught the front of the wagon. I screamed as I watched my dad pitch forward, out of the wagon and between the horses.

It was scary watching my big, invincible dad fall. Of course, Dad scrambled to his feet, cussed the horses, and refused to be fussed over. He was just worried about his hat. He always had two hats, both Stetsons, an old one for work and a new one for when he went to town. The old one always had a wide, dark band of sweat and dirt and he would wear it for years until it was too floppy, too dirty, or too smelly. The new Stetson was kept in its box until he went to town.

The kitchen of our house exuded comfort. Mom's constant presence, warmth in winter, and the ever-present smell of good food bespoke love and security. Every few days, you could walk in and find a large dishpan full of rising bread dough and know that fresh bread would be served at supper. Dad and "the boys" worked very hard and required full meals, three times a day. We had pancakes, eggs, and bacon for breakfast and meat, potatoes, and vegetables for "dinner" and supper, always with bread, butter, and jelly. All that food produced on a wood-burning cast-iron stove was a huge job.

Teta and I helped Mom with household chores. Mom was a meticulous housekeeper. We never mopped the floors—we scrubbed them on hands and knees. We hand waxed the rough wooden floors and hand buffed them until they were smooth and shiny. Eventually, Mom re-covered most of them with linoleum.

On laundry day, Mom started by boiling all the white pieces with lye soap until they were stark white. The smallest stain was unacceptable. After that, they'd be washed in a washing machine run by a gasoline motor. It had a wringer attached to squeeze most of the water out of the clothes and once, my sister-in-law caught her long hair in it. I still love the smell of freshly washed clothes dried in the open air. In winter, the laundry would freeze. We'd bring them inside and laugh when the boys' jeans stood up by themselves.

We had to iron everything, from Dad's handkerchiefs, sheets, and pillow cases to the boys' jeans. Over the years, we went from using flat irons heated on the stove to an iron powered by liquid fuel. It was always hot!

Of all the chores we did, washing dishes was the most disliked. Teta and I always argued about it. Who would wash and who would wipe? Who would clear the table and who would put the dishes away? The controversy never ended.

One day, the usual argument escalated into a pushing match because Mom and Dad had gone into town and Teta was left in charge. I refused to do what she said and ran out of the house and down the road with Teta right behind me. As I ran toward the barn, I ran through a patch of tall grass. Suddenly, a small calf jumped up in front of me. It had been hidden there by its mother who was nearby. The cow, whose name was Yellow, was one of our regular milk cows. She did not appreciate my outing her calf and immediately came running toward me. My brothers had always told me not to run from an animal. I turned around, looked Yellow in the eyes, and expected her to stop. She continued to run at me. Startled, I turned around and ran as fast as I could until I reached the farm machinery. After that day, Yellow never forgave me and would chase me as soon as she saw me.

The kitchen also provided a safe and private place to take a bath. We had a large (about three feet in diameter) washtub that served the purpose. As we grew, we were a little crunched, but it wasn't impossible. During the summer, we mostly bathed in the river. We'd go far enough down river to get away from the Big White and the chalky water. I loved those bathing trips because Mom and Dad would go with us and it became a family outing.

We had an outhouse that caused great inconvenience at night and in winter. Teta and I shared a room and a bed. She would wake me up and say, "Go with me to the can."

I didn't want to get out of bed, especially if it was cold, and I'd say no. She'd wait and then she would say, "If you go with me, I'll make you some doll clothes."

If I still refused, she would get specific about how the clothes would look.

"I'll make a dress with ruffles and an apron," or she'd say, "I'll make a cute little hat."

I always wanted to believe her promises, but I never did get my doll clothes.

I loved the farm. One of my chores was to feed the chickens and gather eggs. It could be dangerous when the hens were nesting. Nesting means they were sitting on their eggs continuously, trying to hatch them and we didn't particularly want baby chicks. They would peck my hands when I tried to reach under them. Mom would just put a hand on their back and quickly reach under them to get the egg.

I loved the springtime when Mom would send for new baby chicks through the mail. They came in three-foot by three-foot boxes, cheeping all the way. Mom would have gotten the milk room ready for them. It was a small room off the back porch, normally just used to house the milk separator. Mom would light a small kerosene heater to keep them warm. As we took the tiny chicks out of the boxes, Mom lifted them out in double handfuls. I would lift them one at a time, treasuring each soft, downy body.

The floor was covered with newspaper and changed every day. The chicks had their own specially treated water and food. If any chick got hurt or sick, we had to take it out and put it in a separate box in the house. Injured chicks would be quickly pecked to death by the others. The chicks stayed in the milk room until they began to get real feathers. They were so cute I never minded the work that came with them.

By fall, the chicks were grown and we began the process of turning them into food. Mom cut off the heads and gutted them. Teta and I had to dunk them in boiling water and pluck all the feathers off. Once they were butchered, Mom took some of them to town and either sold them or had them frozen. Others were cooked and canned for winter food.

Our life on the farm reflected the general mores of the day. Men and women had different roles to fill and different expectations. I never had to milk cows. That was the boys' job. We girls occasionally had to drive the tractor, but Dad never let us drive the family car. Even Mom never really learned to drive. We were all expected to respect one another and to dress modestly. On cold, winter mornings, we had to be fully dressed before we appeared downstairs to enjoy the warmth of the pot-bellied stove. Our bedrooms were freezing cold.

We children had the freedom of all farm children. We rode horseback on a daily basis. Some of it was work, such as bringing in the milk cows, but we were happy as long as we could ride. When my little brother, Jim, was about two years old, Dad would tie him in the saddle. The horse he rode was called Red and was very gentle. Red would just wander around the yard, eating grass and weeds here and there. Before long, Jim would be asleep, slumped over the saddle horn and Red would amble back to the barn where Jim would be retrieved and put to bed.

Although we kept a large amount of hay and grain in storage, there was always a small amount readily available in the barn. The hay and grain in the barn was meant to feed the livestock on a daily basis and that was the kids' job. We had to make sure the milk cows had hay available to them while they were being milked. The horses needed hay and/or grain when they came in from the field. It was an easy job and one that could be done by the smallest of us.

Of course, while we were doing our job, we would also play. We loved swinging on ropes strung from the rafters. We weren't afraid of falling because we always made sure we would land on a stack of hay. One day, we decided to make a real swing. For the seat we used a piece of ceramic pipe that was left over from a drainage pipe. Unfortunately, the pipe was jagged on each end. I was merrily swinging, my feet high off the ground, when my baby brother Jim came toward me. He didn't recognize the danger and I couldn't stop the swing. The jagged end of the pipe hit him in the head and slashed his forehead. The blood gushed and my heart raced. I was sure he was going to die. Of course, there was no doctor available and Mom had to do the best she could to close the wound. I was so sure that I was going to be spanked, but it didn't happen. Dad would sometimes say that he was going to spank us, but he never did. I was sure I deserved it that time. Jim recovered but the scar was a reminder of my carelessness.

We often went to the river to fish and kept an old frying pan stashed by the river. We would build a small fire to fry whatever we caught, usually catfish and bullheads. We never had real fishing poles. We'd cut a small limb from a tree and add a string with a fish hook at the end. Sometimes we'd have a store-bought floater. Lacking that, we just tied a small twig on the line that acted as a floater. We played cowboys and Indians and Tarzan. We loved Tarzan, and we'd swing by a rope over the water and then drop. I will never forget one time when Gib was taking his turn. He grabbed the rope and started to swing out. Suddenly the rope broke, dumping him in the white, chalky dirt just as he began his Tarzan yell. He immediately sat up, covered in milky dust. Jim and I doubled over with laughter and we never let him forget it.

We had the hills for a playground and only our imaginations limited our playground equipment. A fallen tree became a bridge over a roaring river or a ladder to the top of a mountain. A hole under a bush became an outlaw's hideout. We loved to play cowboys and Indians, although no one wanted to be an Indian because they always lost. Although we knew we were Indian, we weren't aware that we were being influenced negatively by the outside world. Gib and Jim made fun of me because I always wanted to be Roy Rogers. I loved his singing and his beautiful horse, Trigger. Gib and Jim said he was a drugstore cowboy. In other words, he wasn't a real cowboy but one who was just pretending to be a cowboy and they wanted to be real cowboys.

We had our own names for each hill and draw.

A cry of, "I'll meet you at sweet cherry town," and I knew where my brother expected me to be.

And the cherries were sweet, indeed. Often, we would not make it home for lunch. I don't recall anyone being angry with us for that. We found our own lunch. Choke cherries, plums, buffalo berries, currants, sand cherries, and wild turnips fed us well. Sometimes the plums were too sour to eat alone. We would chip off a piece of block salt meant for the cows. If my mother had known that, she would have been horrified. Kids eating cow salt?!

Of course, there were dangers to children having such freedom. One hot summer day, Gib, Jim, and I were on our way home from a fishing expedition. To shorten the trip, we cut across a field of alfalfa. In order to get back on the road, we had to cross a barbed wire fence, which we were used to doing. Big brother that he was, Gib went through the fence first. He then turned around to hold the second and third wires apart so I could get through next. I was holding a fishing pole and my attention was on getting through the wires without getting caught on the barbs.

As I bent low and put my right foot through the fence, I heard Gib yell, "Freeze!"

I stopped, one foot over the fence. When I looked down, there, under my right foot laid a small copperhead snake. Terrified, I didn't move until Gib pinned the snake down and proceeded to kill it. We didn't tell anyone about the incident, but I thought my brother was a hero. Another time, we crawled through a barbed wire fence and one of the barbs caught on the calf of my leg and left a four-inch gash. I don't remember how we staunched the bleeding, but I carry the scar.

On another occasion, several of the Two Kettle kids were swimming in the Big White. It was our usual swimming place, and I knew enough to stay in the shallows. As I watched the bigger kids swimming, they were having so much fun that I decided to join them. It didn't occur to me that the river might be deeper in some spots. When I reached the place where they were swimming, the bottom of the river bed suddenly disappeared. I was about five years old and did not know how to swim. I was told later that Eddie Crow Good Voice noticed my hair floating on top of the water, grabbed it, and pulled me out. The next thing I knew, I was spitting out water. We were all too scared to ever admit to Mom and Dad that such a thing had happened, and I never did learn to swim.

Winters were fun, too. Sledding was perfect since our house was directly below the hills. Working hours abated with the amount of daylight so we had more free time. Once we started school, Christmas vacation was the only time we had to be together and it was wonderful.

Although we were poor, Christmas was always magical in my child's world. We always had a Christmas tree because all we had to do was tramp the hills to find one and cut it down. Mom and Dad always managed to get us one or two presents. I did believe in Santa Claus and wondered how in the world he ever got down the stove pipe of the pot-bellied stove.

We, as small children, did have Christmas stockings. They were regular socks that were used by someone in the household and washed. In our Christmas stockings we got a few walnuts, hard ribbon candy, and sometimes, an orange. What a treat that was! Oranges were expensive and hard to get.

One Christmas, the boys got a real sled and I got a cardboard dollhouse. I loved that dollhouse and I kept repairing the tabs that held it together. It was a two-story house with a living room, dining room, and kitchen on the first floor. On the second floor it had two bedrooms and a bathroom as well as a balcony/patio outside of the main bedroom. I had never seen such a house. I made furniture for it out of match boxes and other cardboard scraps. Mom gave me scraps of material for curtains and blankets, and I cut paper people out of catalogs. It gave me hours and hours of fun and fantasy. Another year I received a doll that cried "mama" when you turned it over. Gib and Jim were so curious about how it cried that they cut it open to find out. And then I was the one who cried.

For the most part, toys at Christmas were few and far between. We usually made our own playthings. It seems we were always working on a slingshot. We became expert at finding the right tree branch, cutting the rubber from old inner tubes, and cutting the tongues out of old shoes. I always wondered what Mom and Dad thought when they found all those shoes without tongues. We also played with bone horses, which I discovered later were traditional toys. These were bones from the joints of dead cows and horses that we found on the prairie, made clean and white by time and the elements. With a little imagination, they took on the shapes we assigned them. With nails and string, we would build little corrals for our "cattle and horses." Imaginations fueled, we could spend all day playing ranchers, which was all we knew. Dad carved a top for us that required a whip to make it spin. It was a toy that he'd had as a child.

Dad told us that he had a black crow for a pet when he was a child and that he had split its tongue and taught it to talk. Believing that, we caught a sparrow and tried to split its tiny tongue, hoping it would talk. Fortunately, the sparrow was too small. We couldn't even grasp its tongue much less split it. Dad laughed when we told him what we'd tried to do.

We also used copper wire to form the shapes of little men and objects such as saddles. The wretched gumbo that became our enemy when it rained could also be a resource for play. I was adept at forming clay shapes of little people and furniture for them, but they always fell apart when they dried out.

My brothers Bob and Doc went to war in 1943. Mom and Dad threw a big party when they were going to leave. We knew they would be going overseas, and we were both proud and scared. I remember the party so well. The living room and dining room were cleared of furniture and turned into a dance floor. I was five years old and my dad stood me on his toes and danced with me. Bob would go into the marine corps and Doc, the army. Dad was enormously proud that his boys would follow in his footsteps in defending our country.

In our house, everyone was always aware of politics.

I was very young when I went running outside where Dad was splitting firewood to tell him, "Daddy, Mom said to tell you the Russians are our friends now."

It was during World War II, probably 1942, and the Russians had joined the war against Germany. I also remember lying on my stomach on the floor in front of the radio, listening to the Democratic Convention and keeping a tally as the delegate count took place. It was no surprise when my brother Bob came home from the war and was urged by Dad to run for tribal council. He would later become tribal president five times. Mom was not immune; records indicate that she often spoke at community meetings and was elected community secretary. I have been wont to say that we ate politics for breakfast.

When I turned five, there were so many children in the valley, it was decided that we would have a day school. By that time my brother Johnny was attending the government boarding school. My sister, Deed, had graduated from high school and had taken a job so she wouldn't have to leave Rosebud. Teewee continued in day school in Rosebud and Teta was also in boarding school. My brother Gib and I went to the day school at Two Kettle. Baby brother Jim so missed us that he would sneak away from the house and could often be found, standing on tip-toe, peeking in the window of the front door of the house that served as our school room.

It was a typical one-room school, with desks, but lacking blackboards or other amenities of a real school. We had a good teacher, Mrs. Monroe. Her husband, Paul, was the Boss Farmer of Two Kettle.

I was the youngest child in the school and the only first-grader. I learned to read rapidly and was rewarded by the extra attention of

Mrs. Monroe, who thought it was cute that I learned so easily. I loved school. We had no playground equipment, but there were trees around the house that served the purpose. The following year, Mrs. Monroe left us to become a teacher in town. The day school was closed and the day came when I had to go to boarding school.

Three

BOARDING SCHOOL

I have a sharp and clear memory of waking in the dark, getting dressed, and going out into crisp, fall air. We climbed into the wagon and snuggled into the hay and blankets. It was only three miles or so to the highway, but it took quite a while by horse and wagon. We were warm and cozy as we rode through the dark. The creak of harness leather and the muffled thud of horses' hooves eased me back into intermittent sleep. I woke to find myself looking at the sky. I watched the stars slowly fade and the sky begin to show light at the horizon. It was daybreak by the time we arrived at the highway.

Gib, Jim, and I jumped out of the wagon and ran to explore while we waited for the bus. Johnny and Teta sat in the wagon, wrapped in blankets. I would guess they were sad at leaving home, but glad to be seeing their friends again. We ran in and out of the brush and climbed trees when we were out of Mom's and Dad's sight. We dangled our fingers in the ripples of the Little White River and skipped rocks across the river. Gib was always better at it than I. I watched him in awe as he threw. The rocks would skip three or four times and nearly span the river. It was a beautiful time of the year. The cottonwood trees were turning to gold and the sumac burnished the draws with red. The wild grapes were not yet ready for picking. We knew better than to try eating them before the first hard frost. Eaten before that, the grapes would cause your lips and mouth to peel and become sore.

We played, unaware of the passing of time.

Too soon, I heard Mom calling, "You kids come over here. The bus is coming down the road."

Obediently, we trudged toward the highway. Our little dog, Smokey, ran beside us with wild abandon. We threw sticks for him to catch and chased him when he didn't bring them back. We knew that it would be a long time before we would play with him again.

As the bus pulled up, we gathered our coats and bags and mounted the steps without even a murmur. No tears were shed and it must have appeared that we were quite happy to leave. The truth is that we were reluctant, but we were also obedient. We knew what was expected of us and that no amount of crying would have changed it.

When fall comes around now, the cool air, a soft wind, and the low sun bring back deep feelings of sadness and an emptiness. Am I still yearning for something lost? It took me many years to realize that I was reliving the sadness I felt at leaving Mom and Dad and home.

I was six years old that first year I went to boarding school. I am a mother now and I can only guess at the pain it must have caused my parents to watch us climb on that bus, knowing that it would be months before they saw us again. I imagine my mother's pain and loneliness, going home to an empty house. How did she feel, not hearing the walls reverberate with laughter (and quarrels) of children? How did Dad feel, not hearing the pounding of feet on the stairs and knowing that his boys were doing chores for someone else? I suppose our going off to boarding school brought some measure of relief because they didn't have to worry about food or clothing for us for the next nine months. Sending us away was not their choice. Their choice was that we would be educated and there was no other schooling available for Indian kids. It was government or church boarding school or suffer government sanctions. We were told that Mom and Dad would go to jail if we didn't go to school.

I was a quiet kid. I loved to read and spent a lot of time in my room at home, reading. I was obedient, too. I did my chores and went quietly about my child's life. That life included my sisters and brothers. Gib was two years older than I, and Jim was three years younger. The three of us were inseparable as children. All of that changed at boarding school.

The Rosebud Boarding School and others like it were built by the United States government to educate Indian children, to socialize them, and to separate them from their culture. Federal Indian policy, beginning in the 1800s, was to assimilate all Indians into American society. My parents had already been through the system and did their best to do the right thing.

At boarding school, I found myself in a different world. Arriving at the school, what I saw were huge, cold, red brick buildings set in a square pattern. The girls' building, school building, and the boys' building made up the northern boundary of the quadrangle. The eastern border consisted of the dining hall and staff housing. The gymnasium occupied most of the southern part of the "quad," and staff housing completed the square.

In the middle of the quad there was a flagpole set on a square pedestal of steps. The youngest children were forbidden to leave the vicinity of their dormitories except to eat or go to school, and we were strictly prohibited from going near the flagpole where the older students gathered in their free time.

What I didn't know at the time was that the school included many outbuildings. It was a vocational school to teach farming and animal husbandry. The male students worked on the small farm, which provided some produce and meat for the student body.

Girls were taught to cook by working in the kitchen and dining room. It was considered a posh job because you had access to extra food and luxuries such as cream and butter. If you didn't have a "long reach" at meal time, you could leave the table hungry. The girls also learned to weave and sew. My sister wove the woolen material for her graduation suit, cut it, and sewed it as her "final" for graduation. She remained bitter for years that her academic education was so lacking as a result of her years at boarding school. Learning to sew was not enough for her to achieve her dreams.

During this time, wartime, rationing was the law. There were shortages of goods that were imported into the United States and other goods that were needed in the war effort. Every person was allotted a certain amount of rationed goods every month. We each had our own ration book that contained little coupons that were removed when the item was purchased. The coupons weren't used instead of money; instead, they gave permission to buy certain items. If you didn't have a coupon for the item, you couldn't buy it. At home, ration coupons were interchangeable among family members. Mom would gather the sugar coupons together to buy a large amount that she then used for the family. If one child needed shoes and lacked a shoe coupon, Mom would take a coupon from someone else's ration book.

Everyone was expected to contribute to the war effort. I felt guilty when we used a piece of inner tube for our slingshots because rubber was on the list of shortages. We, as kids, gathered every bit of stray metal there was including copper wire.

Our brothers were fighting and we needed to help too. By this time, Bob was on Midway Island and Doc was fighting in France. I have no doubt that Bob considered himself the ultimate Lakota warrior. He was a marine, proud and strong.

Doc was kind and gentle and I've always wondered how he felt when he was forced to kill. When he came home, like so many other Indian men, he began drinking. I remember him talking to Mom about his dream of going to seminary to become an Episcopal priest. Was he trying to find a way to absolve himself? I don't think my gentle brother was ever able to resolve his issues.

At boarding school, we had to eat oatmeal and cornmeal mush cereal without sugar, but we were provided shoes and clothing as needed. They weren't stylish and sometimes didn't fit. I assume the school didn't need ration coupons since it was run by the government. I remember a time when I had to wear boys' shoes. It was horribly embarrassing even though I often wore my brothers' hand-me-down overalls at home. I really hated the dresses they gave us. They were all made from the same pattern and cloth. The flowers in the print might be different colors, but they were all the same.

We brought our own socks and I remember Mom marking them with our names. I also remember that they would end up with holes in the heels and toes and I'd keep wearing them. On one occasion, I cried and cried because the holes were so big I couldn't hide them.

I did my best to fit in with the other kids. We really liked to get out of bed to play after lights out. There was a particular joy in playing in the dark. Suddenly the beds took on new shapes. The dorm was a great place to play hide-and-seek. We knew we had to be quiet. We knew that playing after lights-out was forbidden, but there was the added joy of doing the forbidden and risking getting caught. Many nights, I was too scared to participate. During those times, those of us who were not joining in the fray would lay in our beds and talk.

The talk was always about home. We talked about our real homes and made up stories, too. We told wild tales of our escapades of bravery and other myths. Eventually such talk led to homesickness. Nearly every night there could be heard the sobs of two or three of us, longing to be home.

Sometimes the longing became unbearable and someone would hatch a plan to run away. We knew that the older students did it frequently, so why shouldn't we? Since we had no real concept of distance and some of us lived hundreds of miles away, it was foolish, but desperation pushed us on. I was desperate, too, but Mom and Dad had made it clear that we had to stay in school. If my sister Teta, who lived with the "big girls," heard that "little girls" were plotting to run away, she would come to see me and tell me not to be so dumb. Besides, I was too timid and scared. Worst of all, nearly every runaway was caught and returned.

When I was in third grade, it was my little brother's time to go to boarding school. He cried so much that big brother Gib felt sorry for him. The school was two miles from the town of Mission. On Saturdays, if we behaved, we were allowed to walk to town. Mom and Dad usually provided us with a little spending money so we could buy a candy bar now and then. Gib and Jim walked to town, bought some pop (soda) and candy and began the long walk that they thought would get them home. They were missed at the first roll call before supper and found shortly after nightfall because they were following the road. My parents were notified and decided to take Jim home.

He was the baby of the family and the apple of Dad's eye. When my parents discovered how unhappy he was, they pulled strings and Jim was allowed to go to public school. He became the first and only Indian child in the school. It didn't matter to his first-grade classmates and he fit in very well. The rest of us would have to wait for several years to be rescued.

That reminds me that once, when Jim was a toddler, he was chasing the chickens in the yard, which was strictly forbidden to the rest of us. One of the chickens was a cocky old rooster. When Jim chased him, he turned and pecked Jim. Crying, Jim ran to Dad who immediately chased down the rooster, caught him, and wrung his neck. Mom thought that was a bit much, but she cooked the rooster for supper anyway.

Every time we played after lights out, we knew we were taking a risk of being caught. When we heard the matron coming, we would all make a mad dash for our beds. Those of us who slept in the top bunks had to be particularly swift. The time came when we played too long or maybe the matron was too sneaky. We were caught!

I had never been spanked or hit by my parents or anyone else. I was in for a shock! I remember the roar of the matron. Those who had been asleep were the only ones who escaped. Somehow she knew who was guilty. The rest of us were herded into the center of the dorm. I watched in horror as my friend—I'll call her Darlene—was grabbed by the arm and pushed close to the one bed without a top bunk.

Ms. Robinson, the matron, screamed at her, "Pull your nightgown up and bend over the bed!"

I began to shake, fearfully anticipating what would come next. Ms. Robinson raised her hand and I could see that she held a yardstick. The yardstick came down across Darlene's bare buttocks, and the sound caused me to cover my ears. Darlene sucked in her breath as the next blow fell. I don't remember now how many times she hit Darlene or even who was next in line.

In between blows and between girls, the matron yelled and screamed, "You will not play after the lights are out! You will be quiet in the dormitory!"

It all became a blur and soon it was my turn. My recollection is that the yardstick stung and I don't know if I cried out. Most of the girls did not, but some did. What I remember the most are the feelings of shame and humiliation at having to pull up my gown and bare my buttocks to the world. I crept back to my bed, curled up into a ball, and cried into my mattress. I lived in terror of the matrons and teachers after that.

However, being a child, I would forget my terror from time to time. Once, two of us were caught talking after lights-out. We two culprits were told to stand in the hall, facing the wall, until we were told we could go back to bed. As the night wore on, we sank to the floor and began to sob quietly because we were tired, but we dared not cry out loud. Several hours later, we were exhausted. Realizing that we had been forgotten, we crept back to bed. I fully expected further punishment the next day for going back to bed without permission, but the matron never mentioned it again.

My first year, having completed first grade in country day school, I was in second grade. My teacher's name was Miss Imoto. Remember, this was wartime, 1944. She was Japanese and managed to escape the internment camps by being invisible on an Indian reservation. We students were terrified of her, having heard wild rumors that she carried various weapons in her stockings and elsewhere.

She was kind by boarding school standards, but she was very strict. Once, she punished three of us, two girls and a mentally challenged boy, with after-school detention and then forgot us. We stayed in our desks for a time and then began to wander around when Miss Imoto didn't come back. Suddenly, the boy unzipped his pants and started toward us. Scared, we backed away from him. He thought it was funny and started laughing. We turned to run and he chased us around and around the classroom. He was older and taller than we were, but he soon tired of the game. Not being aware of the possible consequences of ignoring our ordered detention, he simply walked out of the building. The other girl and I, knowing we might be punished for leaving, stood at the classroom window, crying as we watched the other little girls march to supper. Eventually, Miss Imoto remembered and came back to release us.

Whacking kids with a ruler was standard practice and the only other really cruel action I saw her take was to deny a classmate a bathroom break so she had to wet herself on a daily basis. However, I believe the real reason I remember her so well is that she denied me passage to the third grade, even though I was reading with the third graders, because I was "too immature." I never forgave her for that. The rest of my boarding school teachers were unremarkable so I assume they were not mean enough to stick in my memory.

Outside of school time, life in boarding school was also very structured. Because of the propensity to run away, students were lined up and roll call was taken at every juncture. We marched everywhere, to and from school, to and from the dining hall, and before bedtime.

When I told my grandson this story, he said, "Gram, you were in prison."

Within the residence halls there were places for recreation. The older students had access to a smoking room and time to smoke. The younger boys and girls had a playroom in the basement. The playroom was dark and cold. It had no furniture other than concrete benches around the pillars that held up the building. There was nothing to play with. We did what we did at home—we made our own toys. We used old catalogs to cut out paper dolls and their clothes. We made furniture out of cardboard and played hopscotch using chalky rocks to mark the blocks.

The showers and toilet facilities were in the basement, as well as a separate washroom with sinks for hand washing and teeth brushing. There was also a room that contained small cubbyholes for our clothes and personal items. There was no privacy at all.

The shower room consisted of a row of toilets and a row of open showers separated by a thin wall. I did my best to keep my face to the wall of the shower to maintain the modesty I had been taught at home. After the shower, I was forced to wrap myself in a towel and walk back to the room with the cubbyholes. We were not allowed to get dressed until the matron had unwrapped our towel for a front to back inspection. It was a humiliating experience as it took place in front of all the other children.

The full-body inspection included a search for head lice. Prior to going to school, I had long hair that hung down my back and was braided by my mother or my sisters. I had had no experience with head lice. With so many children in close quarters, head lice were inevitable. Consequently, we were required to cut our hair into a short bob. If we were found to have head lice, we had our heads powdered with DDT. No one knew it was highly toxic, and it was used freely. Lacking DDT, they doused our heads with kerosene.

On the playgrounds, there were swings and a high ladder with a fireman's pole. We used the ladder as a monkey bar, hanging on the rungs by our knees or hands or climbing up, underneath, hand over hand.

One day, someone stepped on my hands as I hung on one of the rungs. I let go, dropped to the ground and my elbow hit a large rock imbedded in the ground. I lost consciousness and awoke to the smell of smelling salts. My arm hurt and when I looked it was bent backwards. I was taken to the hospital in Rosebud where my dislocated elbow was restored.

It was pretty scary because I couldn't understand what they were trying to do. The nurse was trying to get me to put my arm below this huge, ugly machine. I thought they were going to lower the machine and force my arm to straighten out. I just knew it was going to hurt and started to cry.

The nurse would say, "Don't you want your arm to be straight?"

"Yes." I would say.

Then she would say, "Well, put your arm on the table then."

I cried and cried until I finally gave in and did as I was told. I'm sure that X-ray would have gone much easier if my mother had been there. My parents didn't find out about the operation until months later when I went home.

At school, I missed being able to read for pleasure. Books were always available at home. Zane Grey was one of my favorite authors, and I loved *The Boxcar Children*.[1] I also read all the magazines I could put my hands on. Dad subscribed to detective magazines and Mom loved *Reader's Digest* and *Redbook*. Mom didn't know that I read her *Redbook*. She thought it was too racy for me. I would borrow books from our little day school, and I loved stories about princesses and kings and queens.

Even at boarding school, I would enlist my playmates to re-create stories I had read. We would take our winter coats, turn them inside out so the lining was on the outside, tie them around our waists by the collars, and pretend it was a billowy silken dress. I laugh even now when I think of the incongruity of the poor little girl from the reservation pretending to be a princess.

By far, the worst part of being in boarding school was that I was isolated from my family. My sister Teta, six years older, was in the same building, but we were separated because of our ages. My brothers were in another building. They did not even eat at the same time as I did.

When we were at home, I was the baby girl and was treated as such. I followed my brother John around the farmyard, and I loved to hear him whistle as he went about his work. I tried to imitate him and could not. One of my favorite memories is about the time he took me out to the field with him because I was crying about something. It wasn't that he was told he had to take me. He simply wanted to take my mind off whatever was bothering me. He took me with him on the harrow, a heavy iron grate that broke up clods of soil as it was dragged over the ground. As we stood on the grate, my foot slipped and only Johnny's quick reflexes saved me from a broken ankle. He was my big brother and I adored him.

At boarding school, I missed my brother Johnny, and I longed to see him. The older girls and boys were allowed to walk together after supper. They would hold hands and walk around and around the quadrangle that made up the campus. I would hang out in front of the girls' building so I could see my brother. I sat on the iron railing bordering the lawn and waited for him and his girl to come around so I could just say, "Hi."

Winnie Burnette, circa 1940, Rosebud,
South Dakota.

In 1948, there was a tremendous snowstorm. The snowbanks were
so high the "little girls" couldn't make their way to the dining hall, which
was across the campus. My brother Johnny came to get me and carried
me through the deepest drifts. I was so proud that I had a big brother
and he cared enough to take care of me.

The best part of boarding school was leaving to go home for the holidays. Not all of the kids were so lucky. Many of the children's parents were
in such dire straits that boarding school meant their children would have a
warm bed and three meals a day. Other parents found themselves addicted
to alcohol and unable to take care of themselves or anyone else. Going
home for the holidays would have put the children in impossible situations.

There were very few jobs and most of our people were uneducated.
My dad had gone to school, albeit briefly, but left to help on the family
ranch. Mom started school at St. Francis, a Catholic boarding school, but
left when Gram Louise found out that the nuns were hitting the children,
which was unacceptable to Lakota people.

Mom then went to other Indian boarding schools: Genoa Indian
Industrial School in Genoa, Nebraska, and St. Mary's Episcopal Girl's

Grover Burnette, age twenty-four,
circa 1917.

School. At Genoa, she was taught home economics. After all, what more
could be expected of Indian children? St. Mary's treated the girls pretty
well. Mom remembered that on Sundays they were expected to wear
ruffled pinafores and white gloves. She finished ninth grade and took a
job working as the town telephone operator in the little town of White
River, South Dakota. She always worked after that, but she valued education so much that she always kept a dictionary at hand. I remember seeing her sitting at the kitchen table, writing letters to relatives or friends,
occasionally checking her little dictionary for the right spelling.

The John Burnette ranch wasn't too far from White River, and the
Indian community was small enough that my mother and father probably knew each other for many years. At age eighteen, Dad owned his
own pool hall but it burned to the ground and he couldn't rebuild it. That
was his only attempt at any business except ranching. Dad was drafted
into the army in 1917. He was never sent overseas, but he was proud of
having served his country.

Mom and Dad married in 1921 and my brother, Grover Jr., was born
in 1922. After that, Mom blessed the family with a new baby every two

years. We were a close family and were taught to help each other always. By the time we moved to Two Kettle in 1942, our family had already been torn apart by boarding school and the process continued with the last of us. I never really got to know my older sisters and brothers.

I lived in fear most of the time at boarding school. I was afraid of the matrons, teachers, and many of the other kids. Fist fights among the little girls were everyday occurrences. I learned very quickly how to avoid a fight. I must've been good at it because I never had to hit anyone. I did learn that it's better to avoid a bully rather than trying to make friends with them. My friends were all soft-spoken and quiet like me. Unfortunately, I took my fear with me when I went home. I became afraid of my dad who was gruff and spoke in a loud voice. It would be many years before I would be able to breach the chasm of trust created by boarding school.

In retrospect, it's apparent that the regimented living, the loss of caring adults in my daily life, and my own propensity to survive by adjusting to even painful situations were the beginning of a lifetime of self-effacing behavior.

Four

WHAT *IYESKA* MEANS

In the dark of the dorm, confined to our beds, we talked in whispers about our families, our lives at home. Those who knew the language would immerse us all in the mysterious world of Indian tradition and folklore. Like children everywhere, we loved to be scared and the kids who came from traditional backgrounds knew the best scary stories ever. I remember ghost stories, told in English for the most part, but richly punctuated with descriptive Lakota words familiar to all of us.

"My uncle saw a *wanáǧi* (ghost) and he had to go to a *yuwipi* (medicine man)," the story began.[1]

"He was just walking down by the river one night. He saw something move in the dark and he almost jumped out of his skin. He didn't want to be called a coward so he went ahead to find out what it was. He remembered that *Uŋcí* (grandmother) used to tell him that there were dangerous ghosts out there and he should be careful.[2] *Uŋcí* told him there were *wanáǧi* that could freeze the expression on your face if you happened upon them. She had also told him that she knew people who had that happen to them. He went anyway. He walked slowly and carefully toward the spot where he had seen something move. One step. Two steps. Between steps he would stop to listen. All he could hear was his own breathing, the leaves rustling as he passed and a cricket chirping now and then."

By this time we were all quiet, hanging on her every word. I pulled my wool blanket up to my chin but huddled close to the edge of the bunk so I could hear her hushed voice.

"What happened?"

Not to be hurried, she waited a cool five seconds before resuming her story.

"Uncle Joe kept going and then he felt something brush across his face. It was kind of like a breeze, but not really. He reached the spot he was headed for and didn't see anything. Boy! Was he ever happy because there was nothing there. He turned around and headed back to *Uŋcí's* house pretty fast."

"When he got to the house, he walked into the house where everybody was sitting. They all looked up. *Uŋcí* screamed and fainted. One side of his face was all twisted and ugly. He had seen the bad *wanáǧi*! Only the *yuwipi* could fix his face after many ceremonies."

We shivered and promised ourselves we'd never get caught by such a *wanáǧi*.

We talked about dead people, and I related a story my mom told me. As a child, traveling with her family by wagon, they had traveled the entire day. As it was getting dark, they decided to stop and camp for the night. It was summertime and warm enough to forego pitching a tent. They laid out bedrolls on the ground and Mom and others placed themselves under a tree. The night passed and, in the morning when they woke up, Mom noticed that there were pieces of beadwork lying scattered on the ground.

Mom called out, "Look at this beadwork."

Gram Louise told her to look up into the tree where she was sitting. Mom looked up and screamed when she saw, above her in the tree, a scaffold that held a dead body, slowly decaying. In the dark, no one had noticed it. My audience loved my story.

Our nights and days were filled with such stories. We were both fascinated and frightened by the power behind the legends. Full-blood and *Iyeska* alike, we had all heard similar stories at the knees of our parents and grandparents, and it was common ground for us. If the authorities at the school had known about the stories, we would have been severely punished. Telling such "heathen" stories would not fit in with their drive to make Christians of us all. The story-telling was done in secret, partly because we knew it was forbidden, but more because it was fun! And we succeeded in keeping it secret. I don't recall one instance of anyone being punished for telling the stories.

Both Mom and Dad spoke Lakota. Sometime before I was born, they made the decision to have their children learn English at home rather than Lakota. My older siblings learned it by simply being immersed in it at Rosebud. By the time I came along, only English was spoken at home and there were no other adults close by who would help us learn the language. I never learned to speak Lakota.

Originally, *Iyeska* referred to someone who was well-spoken and then it took on a new meaning when the white man came and needed someone who spoke both English and Lakota. These were usually people who had white and Indian parents—half-breeds. The word took on a derogatory connotation because the interpreters were sometimes thought to be taking sides and were therefore traitors to their own people.

We all came to boarding school equally scared and lonely. All too soon we were divided into two camps: those who spoke the language and those who did not. Those who did were quickly discovered. The rest of us watched in confusion as they were scolded for speaking the language. The next time they were spanked, slapped, or beaten. We all quaked with fear as we tried to understand what was expected of us. Who would be next? What new rule might be broken and cause such punishment? Always a timid kid, I became fearful and anxious. Adults were no longer trustworthy, and I learned to stay out of the way. Being an *Iyeska* was suddenly part of my consciousness but I wasn't really sure what it meant, except that it had something to do with speaking Lakota.

The Lakota-speaking kids learned to speak covertly to protect themselves from punishment. They banded together, speaking in low voices and giggling among themselves. Being very young children, it seemed to the rest of us that we were being excluded from an elite group. In self-defense, we resented them for isolating themselves. It felt like they were an elite group even though they were suffering for it. They were the "real Indians." When they discovered that we envied them, they made fun of those of us who could not speak Lakota. They criticized our Lakota pronunciation and made us feel as if we were not "real Indians."

What I understand now is that they were trying to protect themselves and recover from the horror of being punished for being their natural selves. We were just kids but we knew martyrdom when we saw it. We envied them and at the same time disliked them for looking down on us. As a result, there was a huge division between the Lakota speakers and the *Iyeskapi* (non-speakers). It is a division that, passed down through the years, has grown.

Although much has been said and written about the children who were chastised and punished for speaking their language, little has been said about the suffering all Indian kids endured by being constantly battered with the idea that being Indian was wrong and bad. Forbidding use of the language was only part of the plan. Our beliefs and spirituality were all bad and heathen. We would surely go to hell. If you sang a song, it had better be a Christian hymn. No more *Iktomi* stories would be tolerated.

We came to feel terrible about this part of ourselves. We thought we had to change and get "better." Some of us, fearful of the adults and desperately seeking their approval, took the low road, retreated to their side, and tried to emulate them, feeling all the while that we were betraying somebody.

In self-defense, we looked at our Lakota-speaking brothers and sisters and judged them to be less than ourselves. Following those in authority, we took sides against them, called them "full-blood" and "buck Indian" with contempt, knowing all the while that we were really one of "them" and that we, too, were unacceptable. Some of the rest of us were left in confusion, not knowing where to turn or how to act, hurting without really knowing why.

Not everyone in authority was white. There were many Indian employees who helped to pursue this anti-Indian policy, put in this position by their need for a job and I suppose there were those who came to believe that it was better for all of us to be as white as possible.

Deep inside, I always felt badly because I couldn't speak Lakota. I always wanted to be able to understand the stories in the original language. Dad would often tell stories at home and told jokes in Lakota. He sometimes said the joke wasn't as funny in English and wouldn't repeat it. It took many years before I understood Mom and Dad's decision not to allow the younger kids in the family to be exposed to the language. They thought survival in the white world required knowing English and becoming educated. How could they know that our Nation would pay the price for the decision?

As more of us have adopted English as our first language, it's obvious that the goals of the government in the establishment of boarding schools are still in progress. Those goals won't be completed until we have all forgotten the language and given up traditional practices. The government started it and now, if we're not careful, we will complete it ourselves. We were all victimized as children, hurt and wounded by the shame we were made to feel about being Indian. Whether we spoke the language or not, we knew we were part of that group of people called "Indian" and we were all unacceptable. As a result, we did what all children do when they are attacked: we became defensive and angry. We attacked each other, became "we and them."

As adults, we are still protecting ourselves from "them." Full-blood or *Iyeska*, we think we are better than "them." Because of the barriers we have raised between us, we have come to the point that fewer and fewer people are learning to speak Lakota.

We have recently become aware that our language is dying out and that it's important to stop the decline. Efforts are being made to expose our children to Lakota in school. At least on the reservation, cultural practices have become more acceptable. Some of our elders continue to resist and continue to believe that traditional beliefs cannot coexist with Christianity, but some younger people practice both.

Although the schools are more accepting now, it is still a struggle. The educational systems on the reservation are still dominated by non-Indians who are often reluctant to include Lakota language and/or culture in their classrooms. *Siŋté Gleška* (Spotted Tail) University offers classes to educate all of its students in Lakota history, culture, and language, but too many of our people know little or nothing about the facts of our past.[3] Until we all accept our past with pride, it's going to be difficult to convince everyone that speaking Lakota is necessary to cultural preservation.

An additional tragedy in this mini-war is that it has grown to include education as a dividing factor. More than a hundred years have passed, and we are still ambivalent about how we feel about education. Many parents on the reservation still aren't particularly enthusiastic about sending their children to school. There are many who feel that the school is not a friendly place and that they have to be watchful and protect their children from the authorities. Are these feelings and attitudes passed down from generation to generation?

Then there are those parents who, not having completed school themselves, don't see the importance of the child going to school every day. As a result of this half-hearted attitude, the children begin struggling early in their school years. Add the possibility that the family is tradition-ally Lakota and probably speaks the language and the possibility of the child's success in school could be lessened. Reservation drop-out rates are high.

Of course, education has always been easier for people whose first language is English, but whether full-blood or *Iyeska*, people who are educated usually get the higher-paying jobs and stay there pending retire-ment. Since the majority of these people are *Iyeska*, it creates resentment against them.

Getting a tribal government job is very competitive. Full-blood and *Iyeska* alike can vie for them. It doesn't take education to become a tribal council member, so anyone can be a part of the power structure on the reservation. You'd think that this should all balance out, but even the fact that there are many hard-working full-bloods who hold good jobs doesn't alleviate the tension between the two factions. It doesn't seem to make up for the past injuries, and we continue to blame one another for being who we are.

To the detriment of the tribe as a whole, the two factions are at odds, unable to see beyond our defensive postures of old. We continue to be unable to accept the idea that each of us can contribute our tal-ents to the betterment of all of us. It's difficult for the older generation to change their point of view about all that has happened to us over the years. Cognitively, we know we should be proud of who we are, but we've brought our boarding school trappings with us. Way back in our minds we "remember" that speaking Lakota and being Indian are wrong. We maintain our boarding school attitudes toward each other and we're still defensive. The full-bloods (Lakota speakers) still nurture their racial pride by making fun of *Iyeskapi*. *Iyeskapi* still look down their noses and criticize full-bloods, all the while being secretly envious. The worst thing that can happen is that we continue to pass these issues on to our children. We must begin by learning our history in order to understand that we're all in pain and we need to be good to one another.

Five

RELIGION'S ROLE

Soon after the reservations were established, the federal government, in complicity with well-meaning Christian people, set out to "civilize" Indian people. They knew what we didn't: that if you obliterate a people's language, you can destroy their traditions, their religion, and ultimately, their way of life. They made the decision for us that we would be better off if we were just like them.

The "friends" of Indians petitioned the federal government to allow various religious sects to establish missions and build churches to "serve" the Indians. Catholic and Episcopal churches appeared on reservations and the people began to attend. They were told they would be punished by God if they continued in their heathen ways. At the same time, laws were passed, prohibiting Indian people from attending or practicing the traditional religion. Sacred ceremonies went underground. Sentries watched for the coming of a priest or government official. The Sun Dance, a ceremony of dance and prayer, all but disappeared. Today, we are deeply grateful to those who kept our ceremonies and our language alive during these difficult years. People like my Grandma Louise tried to conform to the white man's standards and in some ways it wasn't hard. They preached brotherly love and she had been taught from childhood that her neighbors were her relatives and her responsibility. Christians said they believed in helping the needy and she knew that whatever she had was meant to be shared if someone else needed it.

My mother told a story about a brand-new bedroom set she bought for herself. While she was gone to visit relatives, Grandma Louise was visited by another relative who was very poor. Seeing a need, she didn't think twice about giving away Mom's bedroom set. Mom was upset, but she understood. Such was the nature of the Lakota way of life.

Sharing the wealth extended even to children. If you had more than one child and your sister, cousin, or neighbor had none, you shared. Grandma Louise had seven children, of which my mother was the third. When Mom was about five or so, she was given to a white family who had no children. Mrs. Anderson, wife of a famous photographer, bought her pretty dresses and treated her well, but Mom became very unhappy because she wasn't allowed to play with the other kids. She told me that she would stand by the fence that encircled the yard and cry as she watched her former playmates playing. Mrs. Anderson didn't want her to get dirty. Because she was so unhappy, it was soon decided that she should be returned to her own family. Years later, when my brother Jim's birth was impending, Mom and Dad would consider giving the baby to Mr. and Mrs. Damm because they were unable to have children of their own. They changed their minds when the baby proved to be a boy. That always made me wonder. Did they think girls weren't as valuable as boys? Now I think the Damms just wanted a girl, because they did adopt a baby girl later on.

Boarding school was the perfect place to create permanent change in a people's way of life. Away from our families, we were vulnerable to other ideas and mores. Some kids had never been exposed to Christianity, and we were all required to pick a church to attend, Catholic or Episcopalian. Participating in church rituals didn't necessarily amount to a conversion, but combined with an anticipated rejection of Indian spirituality, it would be a powerful influence on future generations.

My mother and her generation, having been the first to go to boarding schools, were immersed in Christian teachings and were convinced that Indian spirituality was the "devil's work." They were quick to condemn anyone who continued to believe in traditional ceremonies. Mom was very straight-laced, with rigid standards of behavior. She would have been convinced of the rightness of Christianity by the additional imposition of the law that prohibited participation in Indian religious ceremonies. It was very important to her that she pass her Christian beliefs on to her children. Fortunately, her aversion to traditional ways only covered prayers and such. It didn't extend to the language or social activities.

I don't know whether she ever realized that the culture was ingrained, couldn't be removed, and was passed on to all of us. I remember a time when my beloved mother, Christianized as she was, provided us kids with a root to chew to protect us from bad spirts. She could never completely cast aside her culture.

As a family, our summers were spent following what is now called "the powwow trail." Mom and Dad raised money by going to powwows to set up a hamburger stand to earn money. We children were not allowed to have dance regalia, but we weren't forbidden to dance either.

Late in her life, Mom would resume doing beadwork. She would make earrings and necklaces and fussed over learning new patterns, although she never tried to make any clothing or moccasins. I wonder now whether the clash between her Christian beliefs and her Lakota upbringing kept her from doing all the things she had learned as a child.

I envied the kids who had their own regalia. I loved watching the dancers and listening to the beat of the drums. I remember that I had a crush on one little boy who had a beautiful costume and danced with great energy and confidence. Even now, the drums take me back to my childhood and I feel comforted with a sense of belonging.

My dad, following his grandmother and his father, firmly believed in Lakota spirituality. He believed in the power of the *yuwipi* and actively participated in the ceremonies. He told us many stories about the medicine man he thought was the most powerful *yuwipi* ever. Old man Chips could locate a lost child, heal the sickest person, and call the Spirits to offer advice and comfort. If you were present at one of his ceremonies, you would never forget or doubt the power of the Spirits. Needless to say, Mom would have nothing to do with it. I would be an adult before I experienced Lakota ceremonies.

So, Christianity became the basis of my moral upbringing, but Dad's teachings were always in the back of my mind. I remember my Episcopal confirmation. I doubt that I understood the intended gravity of the ceremony since I was only ten or eleven. Mom and Dad were there for the auspicious occasion since the bishop was making his yearly appearance. I had a brand-new dress and my hair had a special "do." My dress was very special and I only wore it that once. It hung in my closet afterwards and I would often just look at it because I grew so fast that summer and it didn't fit anymore. Eventually, Mom gave it away. It was yellow taffeta with puffed sleeves. It had a white organdy overskirt with a ruffled organdy bib and straps that crossed in the back. My sister Teta did my hair. She decided I needed a "perm." Unfortunately, she left the curling chemicals in too long and my head looked like a Chore Girl scrubbing pad with tight, red, springy curls. When I saw myself in the mirror, I cried my heart out, and tried to get out of going to the ceremony. Threats from Teta, urging from Mom and Dad, and the beautiful dress made me go. I never let my sister do my hair again.

In the town of Mission there still stands the Episcopal Church my father helped to build as a young man. It is made of blocks of stone and must have been considered splendid in its time. It still houses beautiful stained-glass windows and although the bell rings no more, I still have memories there: my father's funeral in 1970 with standing-room-only crowds, people standing on the steps and lawn, and my tough marine nephew standing guard at his casket through the night, tears in his eyes.

In this little church, I experienced an unforgettable, dreamlike Christmas ceremony. Mom and Dad picked us up at school for Christmas break and we drove to the church. The church was packed! We found seats and waited for the service to start. The organ began to play "Joy to the World," and an altar boy appeared walking down the aisle, wearing a black cassock with a white surplice over it and carrying a large candle. He led a procession of priests and more altar boys with candles. Once they all assembled themselves within the sanctuary in their proper positions, the altar boys passed among the people and dispersed small candles with hand-protecting paper collars. The usual Christmas service then took place, including the sacrament and traditional Christmas carols. When the service was all but completed, upon the beginning of the rendition of the final hymn, the altar boys carried lighted candles to the people and began the lighting of each person's candle. Each person receiving a light then passed it to their neighbor until every candle was alight. The house lights were extinguished, and a magical atmosphere descended on all of us. We were enraptured and sang in hushed voices. It was an occasion to capture the imagination of a young girl, and I can't say that I ever experienced another like it.

As I grew older, religion became an enigma for me and I began searching for my own truth without realizing it. I started from my own beginning, the Episcopal Church. After high school, I thought I wanted to be a nun. I spent a day at an Episcopal convent in Berkeley, California, to get information on what it would take to enter.

It was a gloriously peaceful day. The grounds were beautifully land-scaped, and everyone was so kind. I thought it was exactly what I wanted and that I could be happy praying all day. I wanted to serve God with my life and I knew Mom would be pleased. Then I sat down with a lady and she told me how much it would cost for the training and wanted to know if I had the funding. I was nineteen and astounded that serving God would cost money. I was so naïve and so disappointed that my romantic dream would die so easily. So much for that idea.

Six

ASSIMILATION BEGINS

I stayed in boarding school until the end of fifth grade. Mom and Dad
made the decision that would impact the rest of my life. I would be able
to join my little brother in public school. It meant everything to me that
I wouldn't have to leave home ever again. At least that's what I thought
at the time.

I was totally unprepared for what would come, socially and aca-
demically. White River School was a small school. There was only one
classroom for all the fifth and sixth graders. I was shy and scared, scared
of my own shadow. Up to that point, the only white people I had contact
with were adults who I saw as authority figures: teachers, storekeepers,
farmers, and other business people. I had no idea how to relate to white
children. My little cocoon of relationships with people of only my skin
color was gone, and I was no butterfly.

To begin with, the school was eighteen miles from the farm and our
transportation was a little iffy. There was no bus, and there was no possibility of driving our car every day. Mom was so determined that I go to
public school that she sold some land to buy a very small house in town.
The house was a former one-room school house. It had one wall that was
all windows. We partitioned it off with sheets and blankets. We had one
double bed where Mom and I slept, and Jim slept on a sofa bed. There
was a very small portable closet, a cooking and eating area, as well as a
small wash stand to clean up. We had electricity, but no running water.
It was a very temporary place to live during the school week. On Friday,

Author, sixth grade, White River, South Dakota,
circa 1949.

Dad would drive into town and take us back to the farm for the weekend.
Sometimes Mom would stay in town if she had an opportunity to work.

The little house was rather shabby, and I was embarrassed that I lived
there after I saw where my classmates lived. It wasn't a place where I felt
I could ever bring friends. There was a short period of time when I did
"have someone over." The mother of a classmate asked Mom if I could
tutor her daughter in math. We were working on algebra, as I recall. The
girl came to the house for an hour or so at a time and I was paid for it.
She actually lived in a huge, modern home and I don't know what she

thought about our little abode. I felt awkward, but we were in a situation that, in my eyes, made us equals. The house was just one more thing that I thought made me different from everyone else.

The other thing that I thought set me apart was my clothes. Mom and Dad did their best to clothe all of us, and each fall we would get to choose one or two items from the Sears, Roebuck and Co. catalog. Packages arriving in the mail caused excitement for all of us. I wore my sister's hand-me-downs for the most part. By the time I got them, they were pretty much out of style and very worn. When I started high school, Mom did her best to buy some clothes for me that were in style. I had a pair of blue jeans that I rolled up, a circle skirt, and saddle shoes. When I wore those, I felt like I fit in.

Much to my surprise and relief, the sixth-grade teacher turned out to be Mrs. Monroe, who had taught me in first grade. Many years later, my mother told me that Mrs. Monroe had urged her to take me out of boarding school because she knew the academics there were substandard and she knew I needed more.

At White River, I was immediately aware of my ignorance. I kept my head down, my mouth shut, and my mind open. I was afraid to ask questions for fear that everyone would find out how dumb I really was. I had never seen a dictionary, and encyclopedias were a wonder to me. My love of reading saved me. Every day brought new revelations and I soaked it up. Mrs. Monroe set out to help me catch up to my classmates, and by the end of the year we'd met our goal.

At first none of my classmates would talk to me and I spent all my recesses in the classroom. Around the middle of the year, things changed and I began the long road of adjusting to mainstream society. One girl in my class began to talk to me. Although we were never real friends, she would say "hi." I felt acknowledged and not so isolated. When I won the sixth-grade spelling bee at the end of the school year, I could begin to think that I might be on equal footing with these white children, at least in the classroom. It was very difficult because there were always snide remarks about Indians, usually something about "dirty Indians," and I wasn't brave enough to respond. I just tried to ignore it, but it hurt. I knew they didn't like me or want me around, but it never occurred to me to ask to be sent back to boarding school. I would concentrate on my schoolwork and try to ignore the prejudice.

I never talked about how inadequate and inconsequential I felt when I was anywhere but home, especially at school. I don't think Mom and Dad had any idea how difficult my life had become. Mom wouldn't have believed that white people would be so mean, and Dad would have expected me to be angry and to retaliate. I kept my feelings to myself and became more introverted and passive.

Seventh and eighth grade were fairly uneventful. I kept a low profile and did my best to fit in. I tried not to raise my hand too often and still took refuge in my books. Eventually the other students got used to my being there. I wasn't exactly accepted but being ignored was better than the alternative of being reviled.

About this time, I became conscious that there were some things happening in the Indian community that I had never been aware of. Partially from some of the comments made at school, I realized that there was a problem with Indian people abusing alcohol. They could be seen, drunk, on the streets.

My dad would drink from time to time. We frequently went to town on Saturdays so Mom could work. We kids would go to the movie and find other kids to play with. Dad loved whiskey and kept a small bottle under his car seat. His only recreation was to go to the pool hall. He would play poker, which was illegal at the time because it was, after all, gambling, and drink whiskey as long as Mom would allow it. Sometimes he would become intoxicated and we would be entertained by his singing all the way back to the farm.

He could play poker illegally because he knew all the other players very well. Even the sheriff played poker sometimes. In fact, at that time, it was illegal for Indians to drink or buy alcohol of any sort. I remember Mom getting her white friends to buy vanilla extract for her. I guess that's why Dad kept his liquor under his car seat. There was a bar on the main street that had a sign out front saying, "No dogs, no Indians." Dad disapproved of anyone being drunk on the street, and he was very critical of those he felt were neglecting their families as a result of drinking.

Mom would never go into the pool hall to get Dad when she was ready to go home. She would send one of us kids because it was no place for a lady. I went to get him a few times, or at least to tell him Mom was ready to go. It was dark in the pool hall and cigarette smoke hung in the air. It smelled of sweat, alcohol, and dirty ash trays. The poker games took place in a small room in the back recesses of the pool hall. There was a door with a very small window through which they could keep watch for law enforcement when necessary. I tried to make myself small and invisible. If any of those men noticed me, they would tease me and try to scare me. I would sneak up to Dad's side and very quietly tell him Mom wanted to go home.

He'd say, "I'll be there in a minute," and I knew we'd have to tell him again.

Dad didn't drink at home or when he was working, and he was never abusive when he drank. He was a social drinker, which wasn't true of a lot of the other Indian people I saw on the street. It seemed to me, at the time, that a large percentage of the Indian population was abusing alcohol and it must have seemed so to the white population as well. It's difficult to say, really, how bad it was. The ones who were drunk were so terribly visible, while the rest of us went about our lives very quietly. At the time, no one knew anything about alcoholism or addiction.

These days it gives me hope that some experts in the field of alcohol treatment are now talking about the role of genetics in alcoholism. I firmly believe that all addictions are hereditary. I have never accepted the idea that it's just a character flaw and subject to willpower. I know too many alcoholics who are truly gentle and kind people. I long for the day when Indian people stop being ashamed of their alcoholism and accept the fact that it's in their genes and that they can do something about it. I have watched my own family struggle with alcoholism. Some of us have successfully managed to stop drinking on our own. Some of us continued to drink all of our lives to varying degrees. Neither of my parents were alcoholics, having escaped the gene, and only two of my siblings had serious drinking problems. I warned my children early in their lives that the possibility existed that they might have the addiction gene. "Be careful and don't drink," was my mantra when they were teenagers. I would give that advice to all Indian children. I don't want to imply that only Indians have alcohol problems, although that's what I thought at the time I was growing up. Since then, I certainly have seen my share of people of other races who are alcohol or drug addicted.

In addition to the alcohol problem, and maybe as a result of it, I noticed that prostitution was an open secret. I didn't know any of the women well, but I would hear their names whispered or bawdy jokes being told about them. I was very embarrassed for them. There was an increase in babies born out of wedlock and a lot of talk about babies being neglected. Mom was often sympathetic and did her best to help those that she could. Even though such behavior went against her Christian beliefs, she knew that times were hard and that people often didn't have enough money to take care of their families. For some Indian families, prostitution and alcohol must have seemed like the only way to survive. Mom and Dad didn't talk about it at all. Shame kept us all silent and racism, once again, raised its ugly head. Too often, it was white men who used the Indian women, walked away from the resulting children, and then laughed about it.

I didn't get away unscathed. Walking down the street, I never knew whether some white man would make a dirty remark. I cringed if a white man even looked at me. It was demeaning, and I tried desperately not to let it crush my ego. It became an issue that would color my view of myself for many years. I did notice that no one ever said anything derogatory when I was with Mom and Dad. It became my mission in life to prove to the world that I wasn't like "those" girls. Of course, nothing I did was ever enough to make me feel better.

What I didn't realize until many years later was that the virtue of chastity is strictly a Christian value and many Lakota people were not and are not Christian. Lakota culture does not include a belief in God's control over one's personal living habits, including sex. In the days following the establishment of the reservations and the forced acceptance of Christianity, our people became fearful of what would happen if they didn't at least profess Christian beliefs. Prior to that time, sexuality was a natural part of life and nothing to be ashamed of as long as you treated your partner with care and respect. It was common for a man to have more than one wife, and it was acceptable for a woman to leave her partner for another. In the '50s, we were a mere fifty years or so away from our basic living precepts and some of us found it difficult to change our ways and beliefs. When some of our people discovered that they could get money for something that came naturally, it must have seemed like just another white man's custom. They had little idea that the Christian world would scorn them or maybe they thought it didn't matter because white people scorned us anyway. My mom and dad disapproved and avoided those women in the traditional Lakota way. I got the message.

When my class moved into high school, everything changed again. Our class increased in size as a result of an influx of students who had graduated from eighth grade from country day schools. It's probable that some of the change came because we were all older, too. At any rate, my life became a little easier. Among these new classmates there were some who were more willing to associate with me and even to be friends. I look at my class pictures and those innocent faces remind me that they were only children, following their parents' teachings. That doesn't excuse their behavior but it makes it easier to accept, knowing it wasn't ever about me personally. Except for two girls, the friendships were limited. I was seldom invited to social gatherings outside of school. The two girls who befriended me invited me to their homes and made me feel comfortable.

Stazy's father was, as they say, "part" Indian. He was a rancher, but he was never part of the fabric of the reservation and had few ties with the white ranchers of the county. It wasn't difficult for his children to reject the racist attitudes of most of the students. Stazy and I spent time at her house after school, and I adored her parents because they accepted me and treated me like all the other kids.

The other girl, Donna, came from a family that was simply free of prejudice and she was uninfluenced by the racism. Her parents were kind and gentle people who worked hard and raised their children to mirror their values. They lived "out in the country," and my friend had attended a one-room school house. One weekend she invited me to go home with her. The community was holding a Lunchbox Auction to raise money. We worked diligently to decorate our boxes to entice a buyer. When we gathered at the school, I was terrified that no one would want my box and I'd be embarrassed. The boxes were packed with sandwiches and cakes, and the buyer had to share the food with the box-maker. That was embarrassing, too. I didn't know any of them, and they were all white. Some of them treated me alright and some ignored me, which was fine with me. I don't remember who, but someone bought my box and I survived my embarrassment.

Some of the other students would occasionally make half-hearted efforts to appear friendly, but not too friendly. Some others were misfits like me who didn't quite fit in with the "in crowd," and we'd occasionally band together after school. From time to time other Indian kids would start school, but none ever stayed long enough for me to make friends with them. It was difficult because they were shy and so was I.

During this time, the town decided to take advantage of a new government program that would enable them to get a doctor who would live in town. The Displaced Persons Act was passed in 1948 to allow Eastern European refugees to come to America to live.[1] They could bring their families and would be given employment. The doctor who came to White River was, I believe, from the Ukraine. He had two daughters who were slightly younger than I was. Having come through the terrors of war, they were doing their best to conform to the customs of their new country. Walking down the street one day, the two girls fell in behind me. They immediately began to make remarks, in broken English, about Indians. I was astounded that these foreigners would have the temerity to make derogatory remarks since they had so recently been despised and tormented themselves. They were white and must have sensed the privilege they had acquired just by being white. It didn't bother me too much because I felt sorry for them because I knew they were worse off than I was.

It was during my freshman year that my sister, Teta, created a crisis in my life without ever intending it. She became pregnant out of wedlock. It was 1952 and my parents were embarrassed and horrified. They sent her away to California to have her baby. The intent was that the baby would be adopted and no one would ever know. The shame overwhelmed us.

The reason it became a crisis for me was that my father was so angry and worried that he began to assume that I would be the next one to shame him. If I came home a few minutes late he would yell and accuse me of being somewhere with a boy. Little did he know that I didn't know any boys that I could be with. I was hurt and very defensive. Being fifteen, I began to see my dad as being mean and unfair. I thought he hated me and I wanted desperately to leave home. On the other hand, the one thing I was certain of was that I had to finish school in order to be really free. I had to be able to take care of myself. That was my mantra when I was unhappy. I stayed in school and eventually my sister came home with her baby, who was accepted and very loved by everyone in the family.

I continued to find solace in my school work. I worked hard and I was in constant competition for the top grades in the class. It fed my ego, but I lived with the "knowledge" that I still was not equal to any of my classmates. I did manage to participate in some extracurricular activities. I joined the choir and we traveled to Pierre, the state capital, to participate in a contest. It was very exciting for me because I had never been off the reservation except to visit relatives in Rapid City. It's interesting to note that if any of the teachers had racist leanings, they didn't show it. I felt no discrimination from them. They were extremely professional in those days. I remember our English teacher, Mrs. Patnoe, particularly. She played no favorites with anyone and was equally demanding of all of us. I am grateful to her for contributing so much to my knowledge of English.

Everything changed again in my sophomore year when my brother Gib finally left boarding school and transferred to White River. He was an instant success! He was a talented athlete and all thoughts of his being Indian were secondary. He was immediately accepted by all the other athletes. I remember that there were times when Dad railed against the coach for not allowing him to play enough. Of course, he blamed the coach for being racist and now I'm not sure that was true. It was easy to see racism everywhere because it was, indeed, rampant. Gib struggled with his academics because he had just come from boarding school. His friends and other athletes helped him with tutoring because they didn't want him to lose his eligibility to play sports. He would become the town hero when he made the winning basket in a state championship basketball game.

I remember the excitement when our school won the regional tournament, which made the team eligible to compete in the state championship tournament. Everyone in town was talking about going to the state tournament. It would take place in Huron, which was about 150 miles away. I knew I couldn't go. A few days before the tournament was to start, our typing teacher, Miss Smith, came up to me as I was leaving class and asked me if I wanted to go. Of course I did, but how could I? It would mean finding transportation, staying in a hotel, and buying food, and we had no money.

Miss Smith said, "Just wait and see."

The next day she told me that some of the townspeople in Huron had opened their homes for guests since the town didn't have enough hotel rooms for the expected crowd. She had found a place for me to stay!

Naïve as I was, I believed it when she told me it was free. She also found a ride for me and handed me a $20 bill!

I was amazed and so excited! I was also scared. I would be staying with strangers in a strange town, and I'd have to find a way to get to the gym where the games would take place. I swallowed my fear and went anyway.

Somehow, I managed everything and I really don't remember how. I do remember the excitement of the games and my loneliness. There were plenty of people there from White River, but I had no one to sit with or to share the excitement. I had to be content with just watching my brother play, and I was so proud of him.

I will never forget the magical moments when we came to the last minutes of the championship game. The score was 55 to 54 in favor of Hayti. With three minutes left to play, Hayti's team played a game of cat and mouse, trying to keep the ball and play out the last minutes. White River got the ball after a failed free throw by Hayti. Gib dribbled down the court, moving close to the basket and then through the Hayti players to make a basket. We were ahead! The crowd cheered and stamped their feet, but I sat on the edge of my seat, knowing that anything could happen in those last few seconds. Then the buzzer went off and the crowd poured onto the floor. Gib was a hero, and I was so proud.

Sadly, Gib's heart was broken when he tried to take a white girl to the prom. Her parents allowed her to chum around with him at school, but they would not permit her to be seen in public with him at the prom. My heart ached for him and I cried. I believe he never really recovered from this slap in the face. The rest of his life was spent trying to fit into mainstream society. He eventually married an Indian girl, but I saw him as confused and ambivalent about who he was.

When I think about it now, I wonder if he felt like I did. When he was on the basketball court or football field, did he feel okay about himself and equal to all those white kids? I don't know because we never talked about it.

With Gib's coming to White River, my own social life improved. We also had a first cousin who was in my class and who was also an excellent athlete. I basked in the limelight of the two of them. I went to as many games as I could. Sometimes I was able to find rides to out-of-town activities. It was easier for my classmates to include me because I wasn't with any one person in particular. We all jumped into one car and at our destination my goal was not socializing with the other girls but was rather to watch the play and to cheer for my brother and cousin. I never expected real friendship from them, and it may be that the lack of such an expectation contributed to the continuing divide between them and me. I was too scared of rejection to keep trying.

My junior year arrived with the knowledge that Gib would be graduating in the spring. I did go to the Junior Banquet because no one had to have a date. My sister Deed bought me a beautiful prom dress for the banquet. I never got to wear it again, but I saved it until my little girls were able to wear it in dress-up play.

Sometime toward the end of my junior year I was finally pushed into defending myself. Leaving class and walking down a hallway, I was accosted by one of the boys in my class. I don't recall exactly what he said except that he ended it by calling me a "squaw," which was tantamount to calling me a prostitute. My reaction was immediate. I slapped him in the face. I can still say that he is the only person I ever hit. We were both sent to the principal's office. I don't recall the outcome. Did he have to apologize? I don't know. I know I didn't cry. I was mad but not surprised.

In 1957, my little brother, Jim, transferred from White River to Todd County High School. Rosebud Boarding School had been closed and Todd County became the new Indian school. Jim left White River in anger and disgust. He was an athlete like his brothers and loved basketball. In rural South Dakota, high school sports are a huge part of the social life of the people and the games were always well attended.

During a basketball game, with Jim dribbling the ball, a white man who Jim knew shouted out clearly, "You --- gut eater!"

Jim was humiliated and mad. He would have quit school, but Mom and Dad talked him into changing schools. He would finish high school on the reservation.

By way of explanation, you have to remember that Indian people had always eaten and used every part of the buffalo, including the entrails. On the farm, we regularly butchered our own cows. Part of the process was to prepare the stomach(s) and intestines for eating. It was not an easy or pleasant job and Mom did most of it herself, not trusting youngsters to clean them well enough. Cooked properly, we liked them. They had to be eaten right away and we didn't get them very often, so they were considered to be a treat. Everyone had their favorite parts. When he called Jim a gut eater, the white man had turned a cultural norm into something to be belittled and treated as an insult.

Over time, we were beginning to accept the fact that we were made to feel ashamed of some of our ancestors' cultural practices unnecessarily. Eating dog meat is another of those. We still honor our brother, the dog, by serving him up as part of some of our sacred ceremonies. It is now common to tell jokes involving these practices, but only among fellow tribal members. Once my granddaughter had a cute little Chihuahua and she named her "Snack." Humor takes the edge off what was once shameful.

Gib graduated and we went back to the farm. One day, Mom got a phone call from my sister Deed that she needed a babysitter for the summer. That would be me! I was scared but very excited because it meant that I would be going to California.

The bus ride was long, but I felt very free. Away from the reservation, I had no problem talking to people. I knew right away that the people around me were not biased by my skin color. I talked to a young woman who had a baby on her lap. The baby cried a lot and I soon noticed that the mother was just snacking on crackers and such. Then she couldn't fill the baby's bottle. I had very little money to travel on, but I bought her lunch and milk for the baby. It was incredible to me that here was a white girl who was worse off than me. I would never have thought that was possible.

Toward the end of my trip, in Truckee, California, I decided that I had just enough money to have a nice breakfast. I thought I wouldn't need any more money when I got to Sacramento. I was wrong. When I arrived in Sacramento, Deed should have been there to meet me and she was not. I thought I could take a taxi to her house and have her pay for it when I arrived. However, when I called her house there was no answer. She was at work and I had no idea what to do next. I went in the bathroom of the bus station and cried.

I was alone in the city and I was very scared. An elderly lady heard me crying and asked if she could help me. I told her what the problem was and she took me by the hand and led me to the Catholic Cathedral, which was just down the block. There, the secretary questioned me about Deed and her husband. The only thing I was sure of was that one of them worked at an airbase. The secretary proceeded to call every military facility in Sacramento. She found my brother-in-law and before long Deed came to pick me up. It was the first of many lessons in city survival.

Deed had a very nice house in a nice neighborhood. She and her husband worked and lived beside white people and even had white friends. Walking down the street or shopping, it was clear that things were different off the reservation. I could finally put a name to the way I was treated at home.

I had a wonderful summer, including an actual date with the son of a friend of Deed's. He was cute and had red hair. We went to a drive-in movie, which was a real adventure for me. I was totally inexperienced at trying to watch a movie and fend off a seventeen-year-old boy at the same time.

We lived in walking distance of what is now called a strip mall, and the kids and I would walk there to get an ice cream cone. That seems such a small thing, but it gave me feelings of freedom and happiness that I hadn't known since childhood. Walking down the street without being afraid that someone would make remarks was a wonder in itself; getting an ice cream cone on a hot day was sheer pleasure.

Later in the summer, we all went on a trip to northern California and visited the Redwoods. I was overwhelmed when we finally decided to stop and enjoy the park. Stepping out of the car, the trees soared upward until they disappeared into one another and crowded out the sky. There was an atmosphere of peace there in the midst of the giant trees, and looking up we could see the gentle swaying of the towering giants and I thought I could hear the wind whispering "hush, hush." There were dead giants on the ground. Some were hollowed out and turned into houses and archways for cars to drive through and cause tourists to wonder. We don't have a lot of trees in South Dakota, and I never would have imagined there was such beauty in trees.

We drove to Oregon to visit Dad's brothers. They had been absent from the reservation for many years, and I didn't know them so I was a little uncomfortable. I didn't quite know how to act. They fed us clam chowder with clams fresh from the ocean, a first for me. They were Indians but they lived and acted like white people. I did my best not to act like a country hick. Everything was new and exciting and I loved it all.

The summer ended and I had to go home to finish school. I rode the bus as far as Rapid City and stopped off to visit our Rogers relatives.

My favorite girl cousin told me I should stay in town because there was a rodeo. I called home to ask permission, and Mom asked me if I would like to go to New York. New York? She told me that Gib was going and arrangements had been made for us to go to school there. She also told me that I could go to the rodeo, which was all I wanted for the moment. My cousin and I sneaked into the rodeo that day. We crawled under a fence and she introduced me to some very good-looking boys—Indian boys. We giggled and laughed, and I didn't think about New York.

When I finally got home, what I was told was that my brother Bob, who was the newly elected tribal president, had selected us to go to New York. The trip and the schooling were arranged by two sociology teachers in Cheektowaga, New York. Their class had read an article in *Life* magazine that documented the extreme poverty on Indian reservations. There were pictures of rattletrap houses and little kids with straggly hair and runny noses. The students wanted to help. First they had a food and clothing drive and arranged to have everything shipped to the reservation. Then they decided that it would be important to improve the educational opportunities of reservation kids. Two high school students were picked, me and another girl. There were also two college students who would go, Gib and another girl. Host families were found for us. I agreed to go because Gib was going. I had absolutely no regrets about spending my senior year in a strange place. I knew I wouldn't miss any of my classmates, and I had no senior activities that promised me joy. I just needed to finish high school and it didn't matter where.

Buffalo, New York, was a much larger city than Sacramento and although I was homesick at times, our sponsors made sure the four of us got to see each other on a regular basis. They bought us new clothes and made sure we were entertained. The other two girls were placed with different families in the town of Tonawanda. Gib was placed with a wealthy family in Amherst, New York. My hosts were German immigrants who were very nice, but we had very little in common. Mrs. Gudd couldn't understand why I was so quiet and thought I didn't like her. She was just as insecure as I was. She, too, was a stranger in a strange land. Mr. Gudd was very jovial and would joke around and make me laugh. He worked the graveyard shift at a Chevy assembly plant so I only saw him on Saturdays.

My big problem was that my school was the source of this "people project" and everyone knew why I was there. I felt like I was on exhibit and to be pitied. Were they looking at me and seeing a dirty-faced, straggly haired Indian kid? I wasn't at all grateful for their generosity. To make matters worse, our sponsors insisted on meeting with us from time to time in an attempt to assess the progress of their "project." For instance, they took us to see *Rebel Without a Cause* and then wanted to know how we felt about it. They wanted us to talk about the kids' problems in the movie and all we wanted was to talk about was James Dean, Natalie Wood, and Sal Mineo. We were just like all the other teenagers who saw the movie, reservation kids or not. They wanted to help us with the supposed psychological problems we might have had as a result of living on the reservation. They didn't realize that the four of us lacked any similarity to the people who were portrayed in the *Life* magazine article. We were just like every other child growing up in rural America, poor but happy. They must have assumed that all of our problems would be about poverty, never dreaming that the psychological problems were deeper than they would ever know. They never asked about racism.

At school, I was treated kindly but differently. The girls invited me to join a sorority and I was welcome at meetings, but no social activities. It looked okay but, once again I was on the outside looking in. The sociology class decided to do another food drive for the reservation and they asked me to go with them, door to door, asking for donations. The worst thing was that I was put on display for the student body to get them to participate. It felt odd, and I was embarrassed to be begging for help for my own people. At the time, I was unaware of the depth of poverty on the reservation. I wondered if everyone thought I was begging for my family and myself. After the food drive, I had to publicly thank everyone and I felt like I was expected to be a representative of the whole race. It was an extremely uncomfortable position. I just wanted to be invisible.

I continued to do well in school. In New York, in order to graduate, students had to pass a Regents' Test that measured academic proficiency. I had no problem passing it. I had to give a speech at graduation, and there was grumbling because everyone was sure that I didn't deserve it. They thought my old school in White River (on the reservation) must surely have been too easy for me to have gotten such good grades. It was obvious that they hadn't expected me to do so well.

I don't remember the graduation ceremony except my speech. I was terrified, but I went through with it because I knew Mom and Dad would be proud of me. The speech was something about the peaceful uses of nuclear power, a mandatory subject chosen by school staff. It was 1956, eleven years after the end of World War II, and the world was fearful that nuclear power would become a power for evil. Everyone was conscious that we needed to be aware of our responsibility for its inception. I flew out early the next morning and never looked back. It was another lesson in human nature, and I came to regard the pity as another form of racism because they assumed we were all the same. My personal and familial pride were injured.

Seven

CALIFORNIA, HERE I COME

We went home to the farm again. In September, Gib went off to college in South Dakota. When he left, I said good-bye and told him I wouldn't be there when he came home for the holidays.

He said, "Naw, you'll be here."

It would be eleven years before I saw him again.

My sister Teewee had just gotten a divorce and was at loose ends. Neither of us could find a job, and I was concerned that I needed to be responsible for myself and not dependent on Mom and Dad. I couldn't go to college because Mom had already borrowed money to send Gib, and Dad didn't believe in girls going to college.

He always said, "You don't need to go to college. You'll just get married anyway."

It was depressing because I had no hope for a future.

My brother Johnny, having finished a stint in the Navy, had already moved with his family to California to work in an automobile assembly plant. He was assisted by the BIA's Relocation Program.[1] It was assimilation with a push. Indians were sent to specific cities to find jobs. Qualified individuals were offered training. Entire families were transported to their chosen location. Upon arrival, they were given funds for rent and household necessities and given advice on how to find a job and a place to live. Reluctantly, Teewee and I decided to apply for the BIA program. It was a pretty scary proposition. Being willing to leave our families and the reservation was a measure of our desperation to have a chance at a better life. The Relocation Program worked for some of us, but not everyone. My brother Doc and his family were sent to Chicago. They couldn't adjust to the big city and soon returned to the reservation. Gib eventually went to Dallas, Texas, trained to become an airline mechanic, and raised his family in Dallas. The people who returned to the reservation were either uncomfortable with city life or simply missed their extended families and life on the reservation. Since then, it has become common for some to complete whatever career they had off the reservation and return home in retirement. My brothers John and Gib did just that.

So many Indian people were sent to specific cities that they developed their own communities in each city. There were "Indian Centers" where they could gather to visit, talk about problems, and get references for jobs and housing. For some people, it would be the first time they ever had a job. They didn't know what was expected of them and would be fired. They would need help and encouragement to keep trying.

In the meantime, reservation relationships were rekindled and families reunited. I met relatives I would never have known without leaving the reservation. Tribal people from across the nation gathered together and began to learn from each other's traditions. Powwows became popular because it was a way each tribe could show off and share their dancing, singing, art, and food. We assimilated somewhat, but we also clung to our culture.

Johnny was living in Oakland, working in a Chevrolet assembly plant, when Teewee and I decided to follow him. Eventually, he went to Los Angeles for training and began his career as an airline mechanic. He struggled mightily to overcome his boarding school education, and he succeeded.

In November 1956, Teewee, her son, and I boarded an Amtrak train for the trip to California. I'd have been terrified if I'd been alone. My sister and nephew made it seem almost normal. Teewee, always beautiful and vivacious, chatted with the other passengers and my nephew delighted in charming them. The train was quiet and the seats were luxurious. I knew I'd sleep well in them. It would be a trip I'd remember forever.

As we traveled down the tracks. I was glued to the window. I especially loved the ride through the Sierra Nevada Mountains, with the train taking graceful twists and turns through the mountain crags—huge chunks of rock jutting out and sitting precariously on top of each other.

There were evergreen trees of every species, some growing, only God knows how, out of the rocks. I stared in wonder and once again I felt free, and joy at leaving the reservation rode with me.

Arriving in Oakland, we took up lodging with my brother John and his family. We all lived in a big, old house that we shared with another family. Our landlady was a source of hilarity on a daily basis. She was elderly and eccentric. She dyed her hair pink and wore dresses that were gaudy and not appropriate for someone her age. She was always irate about something Johnny's kids did. She would shriek her outrage in a high-pitched voice and threaten to kick us out. We never took her seriously and called her "Rosie Blose" behind her back.

Within a week, Teewee and I found jobs. We had both worked before so it wasn't new to us. When I was in high school, Mom would get jobs for me, working as a waitress. I also had a job in New York, as a drugstore clerk. In Oakland, I went to work for Pacific Bell, the telephone company. I was thrilled to be on my own and to have my own money. My plan from the beginning was to live in Sacramento. After a mandatory six months of work, the phone company allowed me to transfer to Sacramento. I was overjoyed and moved on my own to stay with Deed until I could find my own place.

For a short time, I lived in an old Victorian house, converted to rooms with kitchen privileges. I adjusted quickly to the life of a nineteen-year-old, living on her own in the city. I discovered that I could begin college classes by going at night. Twice a week, I braved the dark and empty streets of downtown Sacramento to attend my first class. I didn't know what I would do with a degree. I just knew it was important if I wanted a better life and it was something Mom wanted for me.

The Indian community in the city was small, and I soon reconnected with a girl who was my age and who I'd known in South Dakota. She recruited another girl she knew at the bank where she worked and the three of us became friends and roommates in a very nice apartment.

I was very impressed and proud that I had come so far in my life. The building was secure, with a buzzer and intercom to gain entry. It sported a lobby with soft lighting, carpets, potted trees, and a garage space for each tenant. None of us had a car, but we liked the possibility. They didn't allow loud parties, but we had plenty of visitors. It was to be the first of several apartments we shared, with different roommates. We lived typical single girls' lives: working, shopping, going to parties, having boyfriends. My assimilation into white society was complete. I was just another young woman in the city and began to forget what my life had been before. No one thought I was different and I just wanted to fit into white society. It was too easy.

Then one day Teewee called to say she had someone she wanted me to meet. We arranged a double blind date to go bowling. As I recall, I wasn't terribly impressed. He was too short, but he was more sophisticated than the young boys I'd been dating up to then. He was also good looking, with slightly curly hair and a baby face. The most impressive thing about him was that he knew how to treat a lady, opening doors and waiting on me. No one had ever done that for me.

He became a regular visitor to our apartment. Bill and I never really talked about my ethnicity; in fact, I don't think he ever asked. I didn't think about it very much. Bill had no experience with Indians, and he assumed I was just like every other girl he'd met. He didn't know I was a wounded person. He was in the army, handsome and charming. He'd grown up on a farm, just like me, but I would find out later that his father was a successful tobacco farmer and his family was much, much different from mine. His idea of fun always included alcohol, but I thought only Indians had problems with drinking and he was white. There were times when he couldn't remember how he got back to the base after a party. Fortunately, I didn't really like the taste of beer or liquor and coupled with my fear that I would drink too much, my drinking was pretty limited. After a year of an on-again, off-again relationship, we were married. I didn't consider that I might be giving up my dream of college. I just knew I wanted babies and getting married was the first step. I was a typical twenty-year-old, waiting for life to happen.

Eight

ARMY LIFE

The wedding was very small, with our parents and just a few friends. Mom and Dad flew in from South Dakota. Dad was reluctant but eventually agreed to give me away. He and I had a quiet moment just before the ceremony and we both cried a little. I made my dress and veil, and the only flowers were those that usually decorated the church. I only had $400 to spend and Bill had nothing or at least he offered nothing. Bill had only one suit to his name and it was royal blue wool. It was over 100 degrees that day. Bill was sweating before the ceremony even started. We forgot to pay the organist and my eight-year-old nephew slugged my new husband in the stomach. After such chaos, the reception was held in the local VFW Hall, arranged by Deed.

We drove to San Francisco from the reception and took up residence in an apartment in a very old renovated house. Our apartment was put together from an old alcove and part of what must have once been a sitting room. The tiny kitchen and bathroom were wrenched from other old rooms, apparently as an afterthought. We lived on the second floor, and the stairs and floors creaked with each step. Elaborately carved moldings around windows and doors reminded me that this was once someone's mansion. It was in the Haight-Ashbury district, but it was not yet the time of Flower Children. In years to come, our street would hear the beat of sandaled feet and songs of love and peace.

Bill was stationed at the Presidio and I transferred my job once more. Pacific Bell was located in downtown San Francisco on Market Street. I felt very sophisticated walking among the tall, stately buildings and imagining that I actually belonged there. I had to imagine it because we were a far cry from being able to shop on Market Street.

Still, we had a beautiful city at our feet and we went sightseeing every weekend. We lived on the edge of Golden Gate Park and explored it on foot and bicycle. I loved the museums, the ocean, and the possibilities in living there. I had put the past behind me.

Sadly, we communicated very little. We didn't talk about money, our dreams for the future, or children. We didn't even talk about our families or our pasts. We didn't know each other at all. I knew what I wanted— a family, to go to school, and to work. It seemed a certainty that Bill would stay in the army until he retired. What more was there to talk about? It was a time when husbands and wives came together to have a family, and the division of labor in the marriage was explicit. It didn't occur to us that we should be friends or that we should talk about what we were doing or where we were going. I found marriage to be all work and not much fun.

Very shortly we received notice that we were being transferred to Fort Huachuca, Arizona. I was not pleased. It meant quitting my job because Arizona was not part of the Bell Telephone Company. It meant moving to the desert! And then I realized I was pregnant. It was all very overwhelming. We found a shabby little apartment in the town of Bisbee. Without my income, we were really poverty stricken. We had a living room, bedroom, and small kitchen with an eating area. The furniture was sparse, and I laughed because in the kitchenette there was the same white cupboard with the metal sliding shelf that I remembered from my childhood. I was back to using a wringer washer and outdoor clotheslines for drying. My reservation experience came in handy, but I missed my premarriage comforts, especially after my baby girl was born. I hated the heat, the lack of flowers and grass, and the presence of scorpions and lizards in the house.

One night I got out of bed to go to the bathroom. When I stood by the sink I noticed something beginning to crawl out of the drain. I jumped and screamed. It was a very large scorpion. My baby, Terese, had to sleep in a bassinette at the foot of our bed with its casters in jar lids full of water to keep the scorpions from climbing up the legs.

The baby and money problems put stress on our already fragile relationship. It was pretty clear by this time that I wouldn't be going back to work. Our relationship changed as we both realized that I was completely dependent on Bill. Soon I was asking permission for everything, and it didn't come easily. Bill began to be ultracritical and to make negative comments about everything I did. I would respond and we'd soon be in an argument.

Bisbee was a small, rural mining town. The Fourth of July celebration included a log-cutting contest that Bill and our neighbor, Leroy, wanted to see. It started out to be a fun day. Leroy and his wife, Jean, had had a baby about the same time we did. We all went downtown, where Leroy had access to a roof-top view. We packed a lunch and plenty of beer for the guys. As the afternoon wore on, the heat increased, the men became intoxicated, and the babies got fussy. I finally had to ask to be taken home. At home, Terese cried incessantly and I tried everything to quiet her. My last-ditch effort was to try to feed her even though I was sure she had colic and wasn't to be satisfied. My patience was nearly at an end and there was nowhere to turn.

In those days, husbands did not take part in household chores or childcare. My baby cried, it seemed, all day and all night and I was exhausted. She refused the bottle and when I tried a spoonful of cereal, she spat it out. I tried again and she arched her back and screamed. Bill jumped off the couch where he was lying and came rushing at me. He grabbed the baby and swung away from me. Alarmed at the way her head was wobbling back and forth, I started to cry and tried to take the baby from him. He hit me with his fist and knocked me to the floor. Before I could get up, he had put the baby in her bassinet and was sitting on top of me. He grabbed my head and slammed it on the floor several times. I was sure he was going to kill me. The baby began to wail again and he leaped up to get her. Frightened out of my mind, I jumped up and ran out of the back door to our downstairs neighbors' apartment. They called the sheriff who came and arrested Bill.

I started planning how I would get back to Sacramento. I was so shaken I couldn't sleep or eat. Outside of boarding school, I had never known such violence, especially from someone I loved and trusted. All the men in my life had been protective.

The sheriff called to ask if he could release Bill because, "If I charge him, he will be court-martialed."

I said no because I knew he was angry and I was scared that he would hurt me again. Later that day, a priest appeared at my door. We had a long conversation about the meaning of marriage and the fact that Bill had told him he would never hurt me again and that he was sorry. He went on to remind me that a court-martial would ruin Bill's army career. I said I didn't want him back, but I agreed to let him come home to get his things and to drop the charges.

When Bill came home, he repeated his apologies and promises. He also promised that if I stayed, he would get transferred back to California so I could be near Deed and Teewee. I was desperate for the love and comfort of my family and I knew my mother would be flying to California for a visit. I agreed to try again and I never told my family what had happened. I was too ashamed.

True to his promise, Bill was transferred to Fort Ord, California. I flew alone with Terese to Sacramento. During the flight, she got hungry. My battered self-esteem caused me to be extremely anxious. I was afraid to ask for help. I couldn't decide what to do. Near tears, I finally asked the stewardess if she could warm a bottle for my baby. I fully expected her to say no, that my request was excessive. Of course, it was no big deal and Terese got her bottle. Little did I know that this was only the beginning of a failing self-confidence.

After a week with Mom and Deed, I had to follow Bill to Fort Ord. We moved to an apartment in Salinas, California, where I discovered that I was pregnant again. When I left the doctor's office, I sat in the car and cried. Now I would never be able to leave. I didn't feel safe. I felt trapped.

I was heart-broken because I could no longer trust my husband. My lack of trust resulted in the beginning of my withdrawal from the relationship. Even when everything appeared to be going well, I was on edge and kept feeling that any minute he might get mad again. I stopped arguing with him, and his criticisms became personal barbs. He mocked me and laughed at my mannerisms.

One of my mannerisms that particularly irritated him was my culturally induced way of pointing when I had my hands full. In Lakota culture, we lift our chin and point our chin and lips toward the object. Until he made fun of me, I didn't even know I was doing it. I couldn't stop doing it and it became a constant source of pain. My old wounds reopened as I was reminded that being Indian was unacceptable. At first I just tried to ignore him, but the barbs began to leave their mark and I wondered if I was really so inept and stupid. I was afraid of my husband and it began to show.

After a few months, Bill was promoted to sergeant and we were assigned base housing. It didn't make my life any better. I made no lasting friendships. As quickly as people came into my life, they would be transferred out. My life was limited to housekeeping and childcare. We were still poverty stricken and had absolutely no furniture. We slept on army cots and managed to scrounge a table and two chairs from someone Bill knew. We did buy a car at this time, and I took lessons to learn to drive. We didn't have a phone and my only contact with my family was through letters. My second baby girl, Jo, was born and I threw all my love and energy into taking care of my babies.

We were so poor that I started making clothes for the kids. I was so grateful for everything my mother had taught me. I bought the cheapest material I could find and used small things like buttons to embellish them. Sometimes I used old clothes, cut them up, and made clothes for the girls. We didn't socialize at all because we couldn't afford a babysitter.

Around this time, I discovered that I was pregnant once again. Bill was very irritable and became angry very easily. The babies cried too much and my housekeeping wasn't good enough. He would slam doors and I'd cringe. Looking back, I think the pressure of our growing family and lack of money was overwhelming for him. He took on part-time jobs, mostly as a bartender. Of course, that led to his drinking more. He spent a lot of his extra money on alcohol. I didn't dare ask for anything besides groceries because he would yell at me. Everything in my life was out of my control and I was helpless.

Our relationship never got any better. Our conversations were often strained. One day in October 1962 he came home in the middle of the day to tell me he had to leave and he didn't know when he'd be back. He might be back that evening or it might be a week or more. He couldn't tell me where he was going either. He didn't come home that evening so I knew he'd be gone for a while. Since I very seldom knew anything about his work, I didn't get nervous until the next day. Suddenly, the news was full of stories about the Cuban missile crisis. I couldn't guess where he might be and I felt like my life was in limbo.

It was a frightening time for everyone. The wives turned to each other for comfort. We tried calling the Base Commander's Office, but they wouldn't tell us anything or help in any way. We were on our own no matter what happened. Some of us started to stockpile food, water, and other necessities just in case the missiles were fired and we were at war. I didn't have any money for that, so all I could do was to plan where I could go with the girls to keep them safe. I was terrified so I tried to pretend that nothing would happen, tried to believe it was just another time when Bill was called on alert and always came home safe.

In due time, the crisis ended and when the unit came home, it was in the middle of the night. I knew when they were coming home and I woke the girls, packed them into the car, and went to meet the plane along with all the other wives. I was so relieved that he was home safe.

He was not happy to see us.

"What are you doing here?" he asked. "It's the middle of the night. The kids should be in bed," he scolded.

I was very hurt that he wasn't happy to see us, and he didn't even ask how we managed to get through the crisis. His lack of caring hurt me beyond belief. I didn't know what to do.

My third baby was six months old and I was trying to manage a household with very little money. Our relationship was so strained that I was relieved on those days when he didn't come home for dinner. Affection had all but disappeared from our daily lives. I was never sure that his anger wouldn't rise to the level of the Arizona incident. His behavior became very controlling, and I became more cautious and withdrawn.

Sometimes months went by without a physical confrontation. Sometimes it was a "small" push, a look, a kick to a door or furniture, or something thrown to the floor. Just about the time I would begin to think that he wasn't going to ever hit me again, it would happen again and I'd be back where I started. Whatever happened, the threat of violence was there as long as he was present. I don't know when it happened, but somewhere along the line, my love for him died.

I didn't think about leaving because I had three children and I was a staunch Catholic. Prayers and hope kept me out of severe depression. I had switched to Catholicism after I moved to Sacramento the first time. When my mother found out, she was very upset! I found that there wasn't much difference between being an Episcopalian and being a Catholic.

Catholics didn't believe in divorce or birth control, and the rituals and prayers were much more romantic to a young girl.

Then we got notice that we were being transferred to France. Getting there was complicated and was an adventure in itself. It's odd that we didn't go a short way off our planned trip to see my parents. I wonder now whether I was too scared to suggest it. Was I afraid he would make fun of the way they lived? Was I ashamed of them and their poverty?

We drove to Ohio, where Bill's parents lived. Everyone was very nice to me but I never felt comfortable enough to tell anyone about the problems we were having. I was too ashamed to have anyone know that he treated me so badly. I don't know whether I was ashamed because I believed I deserved such treatment or whether I was ashamed to admit I was married to such a bad person. It's the shame that all battered women feel.

Bill's parents and siblings were so happy to meet the kids, and I tried to put on a good front. Bill's sisters took care of the girls for me while I made a quick trip back South Dakota to say good-bye to Mom and Dad. While I was gone, Jannie took her first steps. It was the first time I had missed any of my babies' milestones. When we found out that Bill had to leave immediately and we would be waiting for a few weeks, we rented a small apartment. I was relieved that we would not leave right away because I needed some time to think about what was going to happen.

One afternoon when the kids were taking naps, I stood looking out the window, watching the snow fall softly. It looked peaceful, but my heart was in turmoil. Bill had been gone for a couple of weeks and I was alone. I was terribly anxious about going so far away from home. What would I do if something terrible happened? Who would I turn to? I thought about the way I had been feeling about my marriage and whether I could trust Bill to take care of me. The answer to that question was, no, I couldn't trust him. On the other hand, I knew that if I didn't go, that would end my marriage. After much soul searching, I decided that I had to trust in God to take care of me, whatever happened. I would go to France and do the best I could to mend our relationship.

We arrived in France on a cold and dreary day. The flight had been uneventful except that Jo became ill and threw up. All of the plane's passengers were military personnel and their families. I had plenty of help with the kids. When we arrived, I was tired and jetlagged. We flew into Orly Field in Paris and I got a quick glimpse of the Eiffel Tower as we drove out of town. We drove south to Fontainebleau and further to a place called Chailly-en-Bière, where we would live. The house that Bill had rented was an old, modified mansion. We rented the bottom floor while the top floor was inhabited by a dear, old French lady named Mimi. The extensive grounds, which must have once been beautiful, were now unkempt and covered with weeds. Surrounded by a stone wall that was topped by iron spikes, it became my prison for the few months, and except for Mimi, I hardly ever saw anyone. Once Bill invited some people over to play cards and that was the extent of my social life. Occasionally, I would go to the store where I bought bread, but it wasn't a pleasant experience. The townspeople were not friendly to Americans. Mimi liked us because we paid her rent, and when I went to the commissary I could buy her a leg of lamb, which she couldn't get anywhere else.

On the second day we were in France, I put the kids to bed early to try to help them catch up with the jetlag. I was really tired, but Bill wanted to go out to dinner. He was stationed at the North Atlantic Treaty Organization (NATO) base in Fontainebleau and we drove there to the Noncommissioned Officers' (NCO) Club. Even before we arrived at the club, I could tell that Bill had been drinking that day. When he stopped the car, he turned to me and began to criticize me. He wanted to be sure that I was going to act appropriately in the club. I was mad that he thought I didn't know how to act and we began to argue. He pushed me against the passenger window and grabbed me by the throat. I was afraid he was really going to hurt me and I screamed. He let go of me and I began to cry. I couldn't believe it was happening. All of my bad feelings about what might happen if I trusted him to take care of me were coming true. I was all alone with no one to turn to.

Psychologically, all my emotional pain from the past was reinforced that night. The pain of the moment and a resurgence of the pain and anxiety I felt the first time he hit me rushed over me. All my old fears and distrust came back doubled.

After that night, it became very difficult to act normally around him. I was afraid that anything I said might trigger his anger, and I walked on eggshells. After a few days of trying to come to terms with the situation, I concluded that in spite of everything, I had made my decision in Ohio and I would stick to it. I would do my best to fix my marriage. I didn't realize that I was subjecting myself to a battery of my self-esteem and that I might not be able to recover on my own.

In the summer we were transferred to Naples, Italy. As we drove our little Pinto toward Naples, we traveled through Germany where we stopped for a few days. We stayed in a hotel run by the army in Berchtesgaden (Hitler's playground) and the girls played in the shallow waters of a glacial lake. The Alps were breathtaking, and I felt like pinching myself to see if I were really there. I soaked up the atmosphere, part of which was created by narrow streets that appeared to be freshly scrubbed and were adorned with down coverlets and whiter than white sheets hanging from every window in the morning.

Bill and I hiked up the foothills to a small beer garden where we drank beer and listened to an elderly man playing the zither. If we drank too much, it was worn off by the time we hiked back down. We had a wonderful time, our problems forgotten for the moment.

As we continued our travels, we passed through Switzerland and all my images of Heidi and her goats came to life. The hills covered in green and the wildflowers tossing their heads in the breeze gave me a sense of peace. The roadside shrines to the Virgin Mary were exactly as they were described by the author of *Heidi*, Johanna Spyri.

I couldn't believe it and I whispered to myself, "They're real."

Right then I could immerse myself in the fantasies of my childhood and pretend the world was a safe place.

As we passed into Italy, we had to stop for a train. The girls were asleep in the back seat of the Pinto when a truck carrying a load of peaches stopped behind us. A man got out of the truck and approached the car. We were a little apprehensive until he knocked on the window, showed us that he had his hands full of peaches, and pointed at the little girls. That was our introduction to Italy and its people's overwhelming love of children.

In Naples, we stayed in a hotel for three weeks while we looked for a place to live. During this time, I noticed that Italian children, when they are small, are disciplined very little. It wasn't unusual for hotel staff to step in if they felt that we were being too harsh with the kids. One day, while we were eating dinner, Jo and Terese started playing instead of eating. Bill lost his patience and grabbed Terese by the arm.

She started crying and one of the waiters hurried over to our table, exclaiming, "No, no signore."

He gathered Terese up into his arms and walked away with her until her crying stopped. It was very much the same as being home on the reservation. The children were allowed to run and play without restriction as long as they weren't doing anything to hurt themselves.

Problems arose because Bill had high expectations of behavior from the kids. I tried to keep the kids in our hotel room as much as possible because we'd been told, by the army, not to cause a public spectacle.

Bill was determined that we would not live anywhere near the areas where other Americans lived. I didn't think about the fact that I would be completely isolated. We found a house in a place called Baia Bacoli, on the outskirts of Naples. It was a two-story villa, and we had the upper floor and roof. It was fully furnished and had beautiful tile floors. The living room had one wall of French doors that opened onto a balcony and patio. The villa was built into the side of a hill. There were two families who lived below us on the first floor and they were in fact, a mother and father with a son and his wife. They were interesting because they professed to be communist and kept themselves isolated from the rest of the neighborhood. They were friendly enough to us, but not to anyone else. Everyone else was Catholic and went to church regularly except them. They said they didn't believe in God. However, they were culturally Italian, so they married and baptized their children in church.

I made fast friends with another neighbor, a middle-aged woman named Antoinetta. She spoke very broken English and did her best to teach me Italian. She had a granddaughter named Maria who was about three years old and became a frequent visitor at our house. She was very spoiled and I had to watch her very carefully. Antoinetta introduced me to most of the neighbors and to Italian customs and traditions. All of the neighbors liked to tease me by introducing me to customs they knew would be strange to me, or better yet, shocking.

I remember well the first time someone gave me a tiny cup of coffee. In those situations, I would carefully watch what they were doing and imitate them. I picked up the demitasse cup and slugged it down. Oh, my gosh, my first taste of espresso, straight! Then there was the customary shot glass of liqueur whenever I went to someone's house.

Eventually I learned to load my espresso with lots of milk and sugar, but I never got used to the shot of liqueur. The Italians loved it when I choked.

Bill had a friend, also named Bill. His wife, Kate, became a friend to me although I very seldom saw her. She would invite me to outings, but I never got to go, except one time. We were both Catholic and she invited me on a trip to Rome with the Noncommissioned Officers' Wives Club. I was excited by the possibility, but when I asked Bill if I could go, he said no. When I told Kate I couldn't go, she urged me to go anyway. I knew I'd never get another opportunity and I wanted desperately to go to the Vatican. I decided to go.

It was a wonderful trip. We had a chartered bus, and we had a picnic lunch and drinks on the bus. We all laughed and talked "girl talk," and I enjoyed the camaraderie that was so seldom available to me.

We got off the bus at St. Peter's Square and I was overwhelmed. Rome and the Vatican were everything I expected, beautiful and awe inspiring. The Sistine Chapel was closed because they were cleaning the ceiling, and I was disappointed that I didn't get to see it. St. Peter's Basilica, the church, was amazing. I walked into the nave and saw a magnificent sight. Everything was made of gold and marble. The central dome was so high it made me feel very small. I walked forward and I couldn't believe I was standing in front of the Pope's throne.

About midway through the basilica there were confessionals. One of them had beside it a post that acted as a fulcrum, attached to which was a long pole that could move up and down. The guide told us that if you were at confession and the pole happened to tap you on the shoulder, you would be granted a special dispensation from your time in purgatory. I had a moment of doubt; how is it possible or probable that God would be willing to forgive sins based on a random tap on the shoulder? In that grand environment, I couldn't maintain the thought, but it would come back later.

The Second Vatican Council was underway, but it was not in session that day. All I saw were the bleachers that had been set up to seat the participants. As part of the tour, we were allowed to see some of the jewels that had belonged to various popes. I was astonished at the display of wealth. Gold chalices encrusted with rubies, emeralds, and such were housed in glass cases along with an array of crosses, mitres, and vestments. All of these items were made of gold, jewels, silk, and linen.

I walked around the room and wondered about the reason for keeping all the treasure when the people who used them no longer needed them and why they were not passed down to the successors. I thought of all the poor people on the reservation and the poor people I saw living in caves close to our villa. They could be helped immensely by the sale of just a few of the items. I was flabbergasted by the display of wealth and disappointed in its use.

The rest of our day was spent visiting more churches and all the sites of Rome that we could see in a day. I was overwhelmed by all of the beautiful sculptures and paintings that were present everywhere we went. The Pietà, with the Virgin holding the body of her son, brought tears to my eyes and the statue of Moses took my breath away. The Coliseum was impressive in its size, and I wondered about all the people who sat and watched all the killing that took place there. The Roman Forum was a stark reminder of the fact that our country is in its infancy compared to European countries. I was grateful for my high school Ancient History class that helped me understand what I was seeing.

I came away from Rome with mixed feelings. I was happy to have made the trip, but it raised questions in my mind. Bill was furious that I dared to defy him and that I left the girls with a babysitter all day. I listened to his raving and I didn't regret going. It was the only time I got to go sightseeing.

Everywhere we went our little girls were great ambassadors. They began to learn Italian very quickly. They made friends with two teenage girls named Rosalina and Olympia, who became our regular babysitters. They adored the girls and would come to the house to get them just to spend time with them.

There were no telephones in the neighborhood so people would simply yell from their rooftops to one another. Eventually, the little girls could go anywhere they wanted in the neighborhood. I knew they would be safe because someone in the neighborhood always knew where they were. All I had to do was yell at Rosalina or Olympia who would then yell at another neighbor and within a few minutes the girls would be home.

Eventually, a British couple moved into a newly built apartment house right across the courtyard and I had a friend to talk to in English. Pat and Bill Rowe were an older couple and he had been in the Royal Navy for many years. They had a preteen daughter who was in love with the Beatles. We invited them to Thanksgiving dinner and they fed us Yorkshire pudding at Christmas.

When Jo and Terese were three and four, respectively, Antoinetta explained to me that they were expected to attend the local preschool. All the little girls at school wore white smocks to cover their dresses. I couldn't understand where I had to go to buy them, so I made them. The little school was situated on a hillside below us. It was a poor little school without running water or electricity. The girls thoroughly enjoyed going to school where they could play with all the neighborhood kids. I visited the school just to check it out.

I discovered that in order to provide drinking water, someone had raided our garbage and had retrieved some of the plastic bleach bottles I had thrown out. I thought it was funny until it caused a problem. One day, I was mopping the floor in the kitchen. I left the open bottle of bleach on the kitchen table when I left the room for a minute. When I came back, baby Janet, who was two, had the bottle of bleach in her hands. I quickly discovered that she had drank some. The hospital was some kilometers away and I was panicked. I gave her ipecac, which was used to induce vomiting. She didn't like it and refused to swallow it, which was a good thing. We rushed her to the NATO hospital where she stayed overnight to determine whether her esophagus was burned. She was unscathed.

Everyone who lived in the neighborhood had a small plot of land that they farmed. There was also a large vineyard that appeared to be communally owned. We were constantly bombarded with bottles of wine and tomato sauce. One weekend, we watched while several neighbors cooked and bottled tomato sauce. They cooked the tomatoes in a huge pot over an open fire. In another pot, they boiled empty wine bottles. Once the tomatoes were cooked and smashed, the sauce was poured into the wine bottles. The last step was to cork the bottles. Of course, while the cooking and bottling was going on there was much laughter and fun. I never got to watch the wine bottling because it was done at another location.

In July 1963, President John F. Kennedy made a trip to Italy. When he arrived in Naples, my neighbors went crazy. I couldn't go down to the city but they showed me the newspapers with all the pictures and tried to talk to me about him. They waved their hands enthusiastically and, with loud voices, let me know that they loved him. A few months later, Bill and I were at a friend's house when someone burst into the room to say that JFK was dead. The women cried and the men talked in hushed voices. The gathering broke up quickly. My neighbors were in shock, too. Some of them cried openly and they kept asking me why I wasn't wearing black. My Italian wasn't good enough to explain that it wasn't part of our culture.

I loved every minute of my life with my neighbors, but my life with my husband slowly deteriorated. Bill was in the Signal Corps, which is the communications arm of the army, and most of his work was secret. At any rate, I seldom knew where he was or what he was doing. In Italy, he was away much of the time and he would leave the Pinto for me. I didn't drive unless I absolutely had to because the traffic was horrendous. One day when he came home from work, he went into a rage over something I can't remember. Those arguments were a nightmare. They would start out as small disagreements and escalate into soul-wrenching degradation. He would find an excuse to find fault in the smallest thing. This time, he decided I was having an affair based on the fact that the sun visor in the car was down. That proved, he said, that I was driving west in late afternoon. Then he wanted to know where I was going and with whom. None of my answers would be acceptable and it always ended with me feeling crushed. Gradually, the emotional and mental abuse would become more frequent and spiral into physical abuse.

About midway in our stay in Italy, I had a miscarriage. I woke up one morning feeling sluggish and tired. Taking care of the kids was all I could do. Suddenly, I began to hemorrhage and Bill rushed me to the hospital. He dropped me off and left. I had to have transfusions; when I realized I had been pregnant and my baby had died, I was heartbroken. They called Bill at work to tell him, but I didn't see him again until I was discharged. I carried my grief alone. I should have realized then that the marriage was over, but I still couldn't give up. Marriage was supposed to be forever, no matter what.

Shortly after that, I realized I was pregnant again. Anita was born and became the neighborhood princess. When we arrived home from the hospital, all the neighbors had gathered to welcome her. They took her from me and carried her into the house, explaining that it would be bad luck if I carried her myself. We named her Anita after a friend of ours, but the Italians thought she was named for St. Anne because she was born on St. Anne's feast day. They were so excited about that.

Not long after that, I came to realize that I might have been mistaken in my belief that I could mend my marriage. In the midst of an argument, he shouted that I was under his complete control. He said that I couldn't get away from him because I was his army dependent and would never be able to go anywhere without his permission. He said that I couldn't leave him because I wouldn't be able to manage without him, that I'd never be able to support the kids. He said it so often that I began to believe it. I was really trapped!

Shortly after that, he came home from a night out and woke me by slapping me. I jumped out of bed, startled and scared. I knew he was drunk and arguing or trying to defend myself would be useless. I escaped to the bathroom, which had glass in the door. He demanded entry and put his fist through the glass. The noise woke Terese and she came out of her room, crying and saying she had to go potty. He gathered his wits and went to get towels to provide her with a pathway over the broken glass to the bathroom. I took advantage of the moment, grabbed my coat and shoes, and ran out of the house. I knew he wouldn't hurt the kids or leave them alone, and I was terrified.

I ran down the hill to the highway. It was dark and there were no streetlights. My heart thumped in my chest as I ran and walked for my life. At first I didn't know where I was going. Traffic was nonexistent at that time of the morning and the entire population appeared to be asleep. I had no idea how to call the police or whether they would be willing to help an American. As I walked, I remembered that our friends, Bill and Kate, lived nearby. I woke them up and told them what had happened. I was still shaken and couldn't stop crying.

I spent the night on their couch, and the next morning Kate drove me to the base to talk to the chaplain. I told him what had happened the night before and more about the problems in my marriage. I also told him that Bill had told me I couldn't leave Italy without his permission and that I wanted to go home. By the time we ended the session I had calmed down and felt better. I agreed to go home and try again after he said if I ever wanted to leave he would make sure it happened.

Knowing I wasn't trapped set me free to a certain extent. Before that I watched every word I said, to Bill and to other people. I was so scared that someone would tell Bill what I said and that he would misconstrue it. Now I felt like I could voice my opinion and that I would be able to handle whatever came afterwards. One day we began an argument, which ended with his raising his fist, threatening me.

This time, I stood up to him, saying, "If it makes you feel like a man to hit a woman, go ahead."

He stopped, realizing we were standing in front of the French doors, clearly visible to the entire neighborhood. It gave me a little more confidence that our communications could get better and we'd be able to work things out. It enabled me to hang on until the end of our assignment in Italy.

Nine

TIME TO GROW

In 1966, we flew into New York—or was it New Jersey? We immediately checked into a hotel and tried to get over the jet lag. The girls were six, five, four, and 18 months. We went to bed and the girls watched *The Wizard of Oz* for the first time. Anita was terrified of the Cowardly Lion and hid under the covers. We all woke up at five o'clock in the morning, starving. We took a taxi to look for a place to eat. Nothing was open at that time in the morning except an Automat, a place where we had to buy each individual serving. It took forever to put coins in a slot, lift the little door, and retrieve each food item. It was my first and last experience with an Automat. Later on that day, Bill went out and returned to say that he had bought a new car. I would find out later that he had bought the car in his name only, which would become a critical issue. The next day we started on our journey back to California, where we would be stationed again. Strangely, I don't remember anything about that trip. We did not stop in South Dakota.

Arriving back in California, we found an apartment in Davis. Within six months, we moved to the small town of Winters. I loved the town and the people there. I made friends through the ladies' group of the church. We lived in a neighborhood that was on the outskirts of town and separated from the rest of town. Everyone who lived there knew each other and the kids had the freedom to roam the neighborhood. It was almost like being back on the reservation.

By this time, with the kids getting older, I began to reconnect with my tribal identity. It was always in the back of my mind, and I wasn't conscious of any huge issues about it. I believe it was my innate yearning for continuity and belonging as my marriage and my world were crumbling. I became conscious of the abundance of western TV shows. It bothered me that so many of them characterized Indians as villains who were always killed. I remembered my childhood play when I chose not to be "the Indian" because they always lost the battles. I began to monitor the programs the girls were watching and forbid them watching what I called "wild Indian" shows or movies. I told them we were Indian and before long they monitored themselves.

When Bill found out they couldn't watch Indian movies, he interpreted it to mean that I hated white people and was teaching the kids to be prejudiced. In fact, he was the one who was biased against anyone who wasn't white. He just never considered that I wasn't white until this point. Both of us changed our viewpoints because of the kids. It came too easy for Bill to use derogatory names for people of different races. Even in Italy, he called the people, who were very nice to us, "guineas." I found it particularly offensive when he referred to black people as "spear chuckers." I would cringe, but I never dared say anything. Although my father did sometimes make fun of people of other races, especially white people, I never heard Mom say anything derogatory about anyone. I adopted the view that, having been the victim of racism, it wasn't my place to judge anyone else. I assume that came from my mother.

Once again, Bill's duties called for him to go on temporary duty assignments. When he was at home, he worked as a bartender in the evening and it became obvious to me that he was drinking heavily and avoiding being home. We quarreled often and he brought up the issue of divorce. Of course, I wasn't willing to consider divorce because it was against my beliefs. Within a few months of our moving to Winters, he got orders that would take him on temporary duty to Thailand. It was 1967 and the war in Vietnam was raging. We both knew it was dangerous duty but we didn't talk about it. We quarreled before he left and he sent me flowers from Hawaii. We had discussed the possibility of getting a divorce prior to his leaving. I talked him out of it by saying that since he would be gone for a year, it would serve as a separation and we could think about getting a divorce later.

After he left, I discovered that he had not left me enough money to live on. I stopped making the car payment and referred the creditor to his commanding officer. Then I found out that I couldn't even register the car because I was not the legal owner. Bill had not left me a power of attorney, which was usual for military wives whose husbands had to leave them on assignment.

My concern grew every day as I discovered more and more that I was on my own with four little girls to take care of. Frightened that we were going to run out of food, I took a job in a cannery, sorting peaches. I had to work the graveyard shift, and the only babysitter I could find could only work the eight hours. That meant that in the daytime I had to take care of them myself. I would fall asleep while they were playing. It was all I could do to make sure they were fed and stayed safe. That job only lasted four days, but it was enough to put food on the table while I looked for another. By this time, I was really mad at Bill, but mostly I was hurt that that he cared so little.

I found a job working in the newly devised Anti-Poverty Program. I became an outreach worker, working with migrant workers and their families. These were very poor people, farmworkers in the surrounding counties. One of my coworkers was a French woman who had been a GI bride and had been a resistance fighter in World War II. She was Jewish and had lost most of her family to Hitler's genocide. She was gentle and kind and, I felt, a kindred wounded soul. We became good friends. The job was the best thing that could've happened to me. I stopped feeling sorry for myself and started to think about what I could do to improve my life. I was still very sad and confused.

When I talked to the priest about it, he recommended that I make an appointment with a Jesuit priest in Sacramento. I followed his advice and although the Jesuit couldn't solve my problems, he reminded me of something I already knew. It was obvious to him that I was miserable and had good reason to think that the marriage was over. He reminded me that it wasn't divorce that was wrong, only remarriage.

His counseling that made the most difference to me was to tell me, "You're a beautiful person and you deserve a good life," and he made me believe it.

I went home feeling better, knowing that my marriage was still in trouble, but hoping that I could still make my life better.

In Bill's infrequent letters, he criticized my working. He was certain that I paid more for babysitters than I got in salary. I ignored the criticism because he never increased my military allotment and I knew my girls would go hungry if I didn't work. As a result of my job, I met many wonderful people, some of whom became good friends.

Over the years I had learned to manage on a budget so I tightened my belt and moved forward. I didn't make enough money to make the car payment, but the rent was always paid and the kids were never hungry. I knew then that whatever happened, I could take care of myself and the girls.

My self-confidence soared. I started going out more and becoming sociable. I became active in the Altar Society of the church and made friends. We cleaned the church, washed and ironed surplices, and arranged flowers. I joined Sweet Adelines, a barbershop singing group, with my friend Joan and we participated in barbershop singing contests. We never did win, but we came close a couple of times. We had great fun at what were called after-glow parties, and everyone showed off their singing. I had never had so much fun in my life. I signed the girls up for dancing lessons and Brownie Scouts. It was such a joy to go to their recitals and to watch them display their talents. They bloomed and became more self-confident. As always, my girls were the joy of my life.

When Bill returned in mid-1967, I found out that he had been in Vietnam as well as Cambodia and Thailand. He was drinking more than ever and our marriage was a pretense. We talked again about divorce, but he had changed his mind. I was the one who was uncertain then. In the year that he was gone, I had discovered that I could survive on my own. I knew that I could be happy without him and that my Catholic beliefs needn't stand in the way. Maybe my newfound self-confidence caused him to rethink his attitude toward me. Whatever the reason, we agreed to give it another try.

Neither of us wanted to break up our family. Bill was always as good a father as could be expected in the '60s. He didn't spend a lot of time with the girls, but he did play with them sometimes and was concerned for their well-being most of the time. Sometimes he was harsh in his discipline, but he was never cruel to them.

Then we got notice that we were being transferred to Fort Gordon, Georgia. Since we still didn't have any money, we decided we would drive and camp out on the way. It was summer and the weather was perfect. Our first stop was Pomona, California, where we spent some time with

Don and Anita Hall, for whom Anita was named. Don and Bill were army buddies but Don had left the army, gone to college, and they were doing well. I was sorry we had stopped because Bill became irritable, and it was difficult to manage the girls' behavior to satisfy him.

Our next memorable stop was Dallas, Texas, where my brother Gib was living. I was very nervous because I had no idea what his circumstances were and I was afraid Bill would make fun of him or hurt his feelings somehow. I hadn't seen Gib since that long-ago day we said good-bye as he left for college. He tried to give me directions to his house, but it was too confusing for me. We decided to meet in a parking lot downtown.

When I saw him, I wanted to cry. I looked at him, hugged him, and memories came flooding back. I remembered playing in the hills and by the river and all the things he taught Jim and me to do. I remembered that he was seriously ill when he was ten or so and Mom was vigilant ever after for fear he would get sick again. Dad called it coddling and tried to make up for it by being tough on him. When we were in New York, he couldn't adjust to living with the wealthy family he was originally placed with and our hosts eventually relocated him to a farm family. I had felt so badly for him because he was so miserable and he felt he had to put on a tough front. He looked so much older, but he was vulnerable as always and still tried to hide it.

Our relationship had changed and we were more distant with each other. Our life experiences had driven us into hiding. He took us to his house where we met his wife and daughters. We talked until bedtime and I was relieved that everything went well. Gib and Bill drank beer and exchanged military stories. I tried to get to know my sister-in-law and the kids. The next morning, we left to resume our journey.

Arriving in Georgia, we pitched our tent beside a beautiful lake on the outskirts of Augusta. That tent became our home for several weeks while Bill looked for a house to rent. The fun went out of it because it was so hard to cook and do other housekeeping duties without running water or a real stove. Bill fished every day and I was soon tired of eating fish.

We eventually found a very large old house. It had two fireplaces that we seldom used because we couldn't afford the wood. The rooms were too big for our needs, and we had to buy portable electric heaters for some of them. The girls enjoyed the house because it had a large yard and a small, old shack where they played house and other games.

I found Georgia to be a strange place. We hired a young black girl to babysit one evening. I explained the girls' schedule, specifically when they were to go to bed. When we came home, the kids were asleep in different places in the living room.

When I asked why she didn't put them to bed she replied, "They didn't want to."

It was obvious from her demeanor that she felt she couldn't tell the kids what to do. I drove her home and the reason for her low self-esteem became clear. We drove far out into the countryside, down a dirt road without street lights to what appeared to be a thicket of brush and trees. Her house was hidden in the thicket, a very small wooden shack without electricity. In the glare of the headlights, I could see trash and garbage caught in the weeds and alongside the road. It was more pathetic than anything I'd ever seen on the reservation. I never had her come again because I was afraid the kids would run over her. I remember the incident because I had never seen anyone so downtrodden and it made me sad.

The other issue I had was the gun culture. Growing up, we always had guns for hunting and I learned to shoot a .22 early on, so I was never afraid of guns per se. In Georgia, guns were everywhere and visibly available. I saw guns in every pickup, in a rack behind the driver and guns laying on a car seat beside the driver. It made me nervous, especially after the little store next to our house was robbed and its owner shot.

In terms of history, the civil rights movement was going on around me, but I had neither radio nor TV and I was embroiled in my own drama. I wasn't really aware of what was happening around me. There were a couple of times when Bill was called in on alert, but nothing happened. He did ask why, if Martin Luther King believed so strongly in nonviolence, violence followed him everywhere. I couldn't answer that because I didn't know what was happening.

One day, after we had been in Georgia for a couple of months, I went on a routine grocery shopping trip to the commissary at Fort Gordon. Bill had stayed home to watch the girls. I put away the groceries and started on a pile of ironing. Suddenly Bill came up behind me and began to question me. He asked what I had been doing besides grocery shopping. He said I couldn't have been just shopping because it took too long. He accused me of having an affair and said he had hired someone to follow me. At first, I just denied all of his accusations. As he continued, I got mad.

I told him, "This is the same old thing. I'm really tired of this."

I reminded him that before we left Winters, we had agreed to a trial period of one year.

"If this is going to continue, I am going to leave," I said.

We came to an impasse, with neither of us being willing to back down.

On another occasion, he came home drunk and started an argument. When I argued with him, he pushed me down and then grabbed me by the hair to pull me to my feet. One of the kids came into the room and he stopped. I had to pretend nothing was wrong.

One day his mother called, and I finally told her what was happening. I think I was hoping she could make him stop, but she said nothing. After these incidents, I knew I should leave but I wasn't quite ready. I was back in victim mode and I used the excuse that I had no money of my own and I was afraid to subject the girls to the turmoil and hardship that would come if I left.

Looking back, I realize how isolated I was during my entire marriage. I can't tell you exactly where we lived in any city except San Francisco, where I worked, and Winters, where I was alone. I never went anywhere in Salinas, Monterey, or Augusta.

It was June 1968 and we had moved into a new house about three months prior to that. We got a dog because we now had a fenced-in yard and we tried to make believe we were a normal family. One day Terese and Jo tried to run away, leaving me to wonder if they were being affected by our ongoing disagreements. We tried going to a marriage counselor to no avail. By this time, our communications were practically nonexistent and there were times when we were actually hostile. The counselor suggested we have a casual conversation in the evening and only talk about subjects like the weather or what the kids were doing. We tried but the tension was so great that we just couldn't talk to each other.

During this time, my sister Teewee and her husband were stationed in Pensacola, Florida. We had a phone, but I wasn't allowed to call anyone or to give out the number. One Saturday I was just doing housework when someone knocked on the back door. I was surprised because we rarely had visitors. It was a strange woman.

She gave her name and said, "I'm your next-door neighbor. Your sister called and asked me to give you a message."

"My sister?" I asked. "How did she get your number?"

Bill was standing right behind me, listening to our conversation.

"I don't know," she said. "We're not even on the same street as you."

It was true. Her house was on the corner and faced the other street.

"She said she was worried about you and asked me to tell you to call her."

She handed me a slip of paper with a phone number on it. I was astounded. Bill was really angry and accused me of sneaking around to be able to talk to her. He accused me of calling her and telling her about our problems. I should have been able to call my sister anytime I wanted, but I was too intimidated to try. Now I had her phone number.

Ten

THE LONG ROAD BACK

The end came one evening when Bill came home. I was ironing his fatigues, which I really hated because he was never satisfied with the way I did it. As soon as he walked in, he started criticizing the way I was doing it. I listened silently for a few minutes and then I got mad. I took the shirt off the ironing board and threw it at him.

"Do it yourself," I said and walked away, shaking.

I thought he would follow me and I fully expected him to hit me. All he did was scream at me.

"I hate you, I despise you."

It hit me hard. I knew in that moment that it was true and had been true for some time, probably since the first year of our marriage.

The next morning I began my long journey back to being myself. The first thing I did was make a visit to see a priest. Deep down, I was hoping he would tell me to go home and would give me a solution to our problems. Fate intervened and the housekeeper said he wasn't in and wouldn't be back for several days. I went to the car, cried for a while, and went back to the house with the knowledge that I had no choice but to leave (somehow).

I started packing while I considered my options. I had absolutely no money and the only place I could think of to go was home to my parents. I knew they would take care of us. In a quandary, I defied Bill and called Teewee to ask for advice. When I told her the story, she was livid. She said she would talk to her husband and call me back. She called the next day to say they were being transferred to California. They would leave within a week and they would take us as far as South Dakota. I was so relieved I burst into tears. I was not trapped.

Later that day, I told Bill that I was definitely leaving and he informed me that he was not going to stop me but he would not help me in any way whatsoever. He wanted to know how I was going to manage and I told him about the arrangements I had made with Teewee. Those arrangements included somehow getting the girls and me to Atlanta where they would meet us. After a while, he agreed that he would drive us to Atlanta. He also told me that he would give me $40, which he claimed was all he had. He was obviously relieved that I was leaving and he didn't care how I did it.

Arriving in Atlanta, we were welcomed by my sister, brother-in-law, and niece at the home of Teewee's ex-mother-in-law. After a few days' stay, we all piled into their car. There were three adults and five children and it was crowded, to say the least. Somehow we managed, but it was particularly hard on the kids.

Anita, who was two at the time, showed her frustration by occasionally crying, "I can't stand it, I can't stand it."

We drove to Chicago, where we spent the Fourth of July with Teewee's husband Everett's brother. The chain of helping and caring for family members came to life. From there we drove to South Dakota and the reservation. Needless to say, we were all relieved to get out of that car. Mom and Dad were very happy to meet their granddaughters, even under such unhappy circumstances. Within a few days, we all drove to a powwow and I was really home.

In 1968, my father was seventy-five years old and had long since stopped farming. He and Mom lived in the little old house where I had spent my high school years. They didn't have room for us so we quickly found a place to live. As always, there was a shortage of housing. The only thing I could find was a tiny one-bedroom trailer with electricity but no running water. The front room had what must have been a three-quarter-size bed and a small rollaway cot in place of a sofa. The three older girls slept together and Anita slept on the cot. I had to heat water for baths, which consisted of about three inches of water. We had to use an outhouse, and we carried water from our neighbors. It was difficult, but I was so happy to be free. Mom helped me find jobs around town, cleaning house for several people. It was just enough to meet our needs.

I went to the local free legal clinic to start divorce proceedings in September, and by November I had the papers in hand. One day, out of the blue, Bill appeared at my door. He was being deployed to Vietnam and wanted to take the girls to Rapid City for a visit. I let them go and they had a good time. When he brought them back, I asked him to sign the divorce papers and he agreed. I was grateful for that because actually getting the divorce could have been very difficult without his signature. I was also hoping he would give us some money, but he refused. He said nothing about our living arrangements.

Life in White River was pretty much the same as it had been when I was growing up. Most of my classmates were married and had children. We were all grown up, and as for me, I never intended to stay and I was less conscious of what anyone thought about me or my circumstances. I picked up a friendship with one of the women with whom I had competed for grades. We occasionally had coffee together at her house and our kids played together. She was a good friend at a time when I really needed one.

One day I heard the wind blowing and when I looked out, I noticed that we were in the middle of a blizzard. The snow was piling up in huge drifts and I could barely see across the road. We were only about two blocks from the school, but I was worried about how the kids would get home. Leaving Anita with Mom, I went to the school and found that the girls were bundled up and ready to leave. In blowing snow and deep drifts, we all held hands and trudged our way home. In our little trailer, we were safe and warm.

We were very poor, but our life was peaceful and we were happy. The girls had no toys at all. We went to the little town library at least once a week to check out books, and Anita played with a Lite-Brite they had. Every night I would read stories to get the girls ready for sleep. Of course, I resumed my habit of reading, which I had been unable to do for a long time. Some evenings, after the girls were asleep, I would listen to someone like Glenn Campbell singing "Wichita Lineman" on the little radio Mom lent me, all the while putting together a jigsaw puzzle. It was the first time I'd had any leisure time in many years.

I was independent again, but Mom and Dad were always there to help. Every Sunday we would have supper with them and the kids had a chance to watch TV. We watched *Wild Kingdom* and ate Mom's fried chicken and mashed potatoes. I felt safe and loved.

In order to get my laundry done, I had to go down to Main Street, where there was a laundromat. It was only three blocks away, and I would put my laundry in a little wagon and walk. One day it was cold and blustery so I asked Dad if I could use his car. Being kind of grumpy, he said no in a harsh voice. I was surprised because he had never refused and it hurt my feelings. I went home, cried, and started loading my little wagon. Before I finished, Dad was at my door. He didn't apologize, but he started to help me take the clothes to the car. We'd had a longstanding mini-feud going on. We kept our distance from each other and didn't talk unless it was absolutely necessary. Our relationship had been cool since I was in high school and neither of us could bridge the chasm. On this day, my dad became the peacemaker. Without a word to say so, I knew he was sorry for treating me like a kid and I, without a word, accepted his apology. From that moment on, we were at peace with one another and our love was taken for granted.

In December, Dad drove me twenty miles to the courthouse to finalize the divorce. He told stories and joked to cheer me up.

He said, "If I knew you were going to get a divorce, I wouldn't have given you away in the first place."

The divorce and knowing Bill wouldn't be around for at least a year gave me breathing room and I could begin to contemplate what I would do next.

Christmas was coming, and I wasn't sure how I would make it a happy one for the girls. I talked to Mom and we decided we could make some things for them. Dad went out and cut us a very tiny tree, which I placed on top of a small built-in chest of drawers. There was actually no room to put anything under it and any presents would have to be put on the floor below it.

Mom gave us a string of lights and a handful of old Christmas cards. The girls and I sat down, cut up the cards, and made simple decorations to hang on the tree. We also made red and green paper chains and strung popcorn.

Every evening, after the girls were asleep, I would go to Mom's house, which was only about fifty yards away. She had managed to find four secondhand dolls that were in pretty good shape and we cut and sewed each doll a wardrobe. She even made tiny pieced quilts for each doll. On Christmas, the girls' stockings were filled with candy and fruit. The girls all agree that it was the best Christmas ever.

When spring came, Dad took me to the agency in Rosebud because we had heard the relocation program was still active. I had to take an aptitude test and eventually it was decided that I could go back to California. I had a choice of where I could go and I could choose a training program. I decided to go to San Jose, where I would get training in computer programming. My dreams of a future rebloomed and I had hope once again.

The BIA provided us with a ride to North Platte, Nebraska. Here I was, at the starting point again, back where I had been ten years earlier. Well, not exactly. I had my beautiful little girls, and I had learned some hard lessons. They dropped us off at a rather scruffy motel where we would spend the night. For a moment I felt abandoned and alone, and then I had to look after the girls. The motel was old and neglected. The paint was peeling off the walls everywhere. The bathtub in the communal bathroom was an old claw-footed one, and the enamel was chipped and stained by years of mineral accumulation. I made the girls stand up in the tub as I washed them up. I was tempted to skip the bath, but I knew it would be two days before we'd get another chance to bathe. We slept in beds with lumpy and sagging mattresses. I didn't sleep very much because I was afraid I wouldn't wake in time.

I woke very early, anxious that we might miss the train. The girls quickly became excited and dressed without complaint. We ate breakfast and then sat in the waiting room until the train finally arrived. The girls had a great time, playing in the aisle and sleeping in the reclining seats. It was an easy trip because they were not confined to sitting the entire time. They were sweet and charming and the other passengers loved them. I read and the clickity, clack, clack of the wheels of the train eased me into a peaceful sleep. I was starting over and I was free again. I was free from a loveless marriage, free of fear, and free from the hopelessness of having to live on the reservation.

At that time, Johnny and family were living in San Jose. The Bureau of Indian Affairs helped me find a house, and I started my training to become a computer programmer. Bill completed his tour in Vietnam. He'd had our furniture in storage and he agreed that I could have it. He also agreed that I could have the use of "his" car while he went on another temporary assignment. I was grateful because it made my life easier. We decided to get a dog and found "Ginger" at the local pound. She was black with brown markings. She looked like a large Dachshund, with a long body and short legs. Her first owner didn't want her because she barked too much, which suited us. There had been a rash of house break-ins resulting in rape. That really frightened me, but Ginger's barking combined with her gray eyes made her appear ferocious and comforted me. I completed the training in six months and decided that we would move back to Winters where I had been so happy and where I knew the girls would be safe.

Not finding any jobs in Winters, I reapplied to the telephone company and found that the only jobs available were in Sacramento. They hired me to work the graveyard shift in the computer room of the billing department. It wasn't hard to find a babysitter because everyone remembered us from the last time we were in Winters and we'd only been gone for a year. The really difficult part was driving the thirty miles to Sacramento in the middle of the night and driving home after an eight-hour shift. The girls left for school as I arrived home from work, and the only time I had with them was after school until their bedtime.

I did love my job, mostly because there were opportunities for promotion. I hoped that eventually I would be able to be a computer programmer. In the meantime, I would learn everything I could about computers in general.

The main job of the computer room was to get the telephone bills together and addressed properly. My first job was running the IBM card machine. This machine was about six feet long, two feet wide, and four feet high. It had to be loaded continuously with IBM punch cards containing the names and addresses of every telephone customer. The information on the cards was transferred to magnetic tape. The magnetic tape was used to print the information on a bill. In order to run the IBM card machine, I was on my feet the entire shift. I began to have problems with aching knees and I assumed it came from standing so much and I had to tough it out because it was my job.

During this time, Bill came back after another temporary duty assignment. He showed up on my doorstep and informed me that he wanted his car back. That put me in a state of desperation, but I knew I couldn't keep it. As always, my family came to the rescue. My sister Teta gave me her old car, a 1950s Ford. It wasn't very reliable and became the first in a long string of used cars. Fortunately, my brother Johnny, being a mechanic, was always willing to do repair work. He would explain exactly what was wrong and what needed to be done. I learned to change my own tires and oil, the difference between a failing battery and starter, and when to give up and get another car.

Bill had liked living in Winters too, so he stuck around for a while. It wasn't good. He hadn't had time to adjust to the fact that we were divorced and we argued over the smallest things. He wanted to fix my screen door and I refused, fearing that he would use it to interfere in my life. He was jealous when he found out I was going out to the movies. He started an argument over it, saying I was neglecting the kids.

Red faced and angry, he very pointedly told me, "I have a gun in my car and I'll use it."

That scared me, and I was so relieved when he slammed out the door. It brought back all the fear and I called the sheriff, who refused to do anything because he knew Bill.

By this time, I was enjoying being on my own. I had my own money and I was answerable to no one. The '70s were a time when women were coming into their own and with freedom came self-confidence. I had to stand up for myself so I could protect my children. Some of the confidence was a façade that gradually became real. Bill even accused me of going without a bra and being a "women's libber." Who, me? I was surprised because I certainly didn't identify myself as such. I had loved my life as a single girl and reveled in my independence when I was a lonely military wife. I was simply enjoying my life without criticism or interference from anyone. Looking back, I believe my parents instilled in all of us the expectation that we would be independent. It was natural for me to take care of myself. Submission in my marriage wasn't natural, and I wasn't happy until I got out of it.

The girls enjoyed having their dad around for a short period of time, and they all took a trip to see his parents in Ohio for Christmas. Except for Terese, it would be the last time they ever saw him.

In 1970, my wonderful friends in Winters kept the girls for me while I went home. Dad had cancer and we'd been told he was dying. Johnny, Teta, and I drove through the day and night to South Dakota.

Toward the end of the trip, as we were driving down a two-lane highway, Teta suddenly said, "Look, there's an owl."

The owl flew beside us for a brief moment and there was silence in the car as we watched it.

When it was gone, Teta said, "Dad must be gone."

Lakota people believe that owls are messengers from the Spirits. We rode the rest of the way to the hospital in silence. When we got there, Dad was, indeed, gone.

His funeral was sad but wonderful. I was reminded that he was a pillar of the community. Respected by everyone who knew him, he never allowed the racism to reduce his self-esteem. He railed against it at home, but he never publicly exhibited his anger about it unless someone said something to his face. That didn't happen very much because my dad was a huge man, tall and burly with a voice to match. When he walked down the street in his Stetson, he naturally garnered attention. After the funeral, when we drove the twelve miles from the church to the cemetery, the line of cars stretched for more than a mile.

Shortly after I returned to California, I got notice that the BIA would help me buy a home. I couldn't believe it—my own home! They gave me a $2,000 down payment and I found a house I could afford in south Sacramento. It wasn't the best neighborhood, but I was thrilled to have a house of my own. It had four bedrooms and two bathrooms. An attached garage led out to a big backyard where there was a rose garden. The rose garden became my place of refuge. I spent hours on end pruning and feeding the flowers. The kids would avoid me because if they came around I'd usually put them to work pulling weeds. It was a very nice house and I loved it.

Settling in, I decided it was time to get a TV. The kids wanted a color TV and I went shopping. I quickly learned that the prices were beyond my budget. Never having had a credit card, I had to apply for credit. The salesman quickly discovered that, while I had a good work record, I had no credit record. Eventually, it was decided that they would sell me the TV on the store's installment plan. However, I would have to wait until my credit cleared.

The salesman said, "I'd let you take it home, if you had a husband."

I didn't understand why having a husband would make me a more secure credit risk. I was livid, but there was nothing I could do about it. We got our TV about a week later. A few months later, I applied for and got my first credit card, a JC Penney card. From then on, I had no further trouble getting credit.

The girls started public school and we began to get to know our neighbors. Some of their friends would be part of our lives for a lifetime.

Anita had her fourth birthday and we had a party for her. We took week-end trips to go camping, sometimes with friends from Winters.

Once we camped in a campground in the hills above San Francisco. It was so beautiful and the weather was so fair that we decided not to use the tent and laid out our sleeping bags on the bare ground so we could see the stars as we went to sleep. We were chatting quietly so as not to disturb the other campers when Ginger started barking. A man approached our campsite and "knocked" on a nearby tree.

"I'm sorry," he said with a thick accent. "My wife is sick. May I borrow your lantern?"

He was obviously from a foreign country and uncertain of the pro-tocol of camping. His initial approach had scared us since we didn't have a man around to protect us. We all broke into relieved laughter because we were out in the open and the man felt it necessary to "knock."

We woke in the morning to see fog hanging over "The City" below us. The fog seemed to bring a hush and softness to the usual hustle and bustle of city life. I tried not to think about the last time I had lived in San Francisco. We stopped to enjoy the moment before the girls were off to play.

We didn't have much money but we could always find things to do that cost little or nothing. We went often to San Francisco. We would go to the Exploratorium where the kids learned science while having fun. Golden Gate Park was our favorite place, with the aquarium and all the gardens, museums, and oh yes, the Planetarium.

Sometimes we would spend the entire day at Baker's Beach, which was just below the Golden Gate Bridge. We'd drive through the gates of a stone fence, onto a roadway that wound through an exclusive neighbor-hood of elegant beachfront homes. As we got closer to the public beach, we passed a stand of trees, stunted, twisted, and gnarled by the ever-present wind. It was nearly always cold but we took jackets and blankets. The kids played and I soaked up the view of the bridge and the calming sound of the ocean washing up on the shore.

On one of those trips, driving my 1950s Ford and looking for a par-ticular street, suddenly we heard a loud scraping noise. I stopped the car, got out, and discovered that the muffler hanger had broken and the muffler was dragging on the ground. Embarrassed but unable to afford a trip to a garage, I had to find a solution. The only thing I had available that would take heat was Ginger's choke chain. Don't ask how I did it or why it worked because I don't know, but it worked long enough to get us home. The kids thought it was very funny to watch me lying on the ground, trying to make repairs.

We spent a lot of our weekends with my mom and my sisters. Sometimes Johnny would come up from San Jose and we'd have family dinners just like the old days, laughing and teasing each other. Life was good.

Eleven

OBSTACLES

In 1972, my life changed again. I was working at my IBM card machine and the time came for me to change the magnetic tape. The tape drive was about six feet high and three feet wide. It held a large reel of magnetic tape and a second reel to rewind the tape. The reels were held on the drive by a central hub that the operator could pop in and out as needed. I would put the reel on the hub and then hit the hub with the palm of my hand to push it in. On this night, I put fresh tape on the hub and I soon realized that I had not hit the hub hard enough. The tape fell off the hub, literally destroying several hours of work. The reason I hadn't hit it hard enough was because my hand hurt. I had been having pain in my knees for several months and then my hands began to hurt.

Feeling badly about what had happened to the tape, the next day I went to the company doctor to find out if there was a reason for all the pain. He referred me to an outside doctor for a diagnosis. The doctor was a rheumatologist.

After a thorough examination and some tests, he said to me, "You have rheumatoid arthritis."

I didn't know what that meant, and he went on to explain that the cartilage in my joints was inflamed and swollen, causing the pain. That explained my painful knees and hands. He went on to say that it's a progressive disease and that there is no cure. At the time, there was no real medication for the disease.

At work, I was given desk jobs that made me unhappy because they interfered with my plans for promotion. I was transferred to the Engineering Department where I got my first taste of the "glass ceiling."

At that time, some of the engineers in the department didn't have degrees. They got their jobs by working their way up through the ranks and gaining knowledge through experience. Few, if any, were women. The supervisor of my section was a woman named Shirley. She had worked for the telephone company for many years and had been in the Engineering Department for several years. She knew the ins and outs of every position and supervised about five people, including two men and me. She was my trainer. I don't really remember what the job was except that it had something to do with schematics and I loved the structure and the logic. I also learned to send and receive teletype messages. The teletype could be compared to a very large typewriter. Messages were created by typing, in code, on a paper ribbon. It created raised letters and numbers which were then transmitted by wire. Shirley worked diligently and was, she hoped, on the verge of being promoted to full-fledged engineer. I watched her and hoped I could follow in her footsteps.

The main department supervisor was a man named Stan. He was openly opposed to women being in supervisory positions. He often made crude jokes about it. He appeared to genuinely like Shirley but he was against her promotion. One day, Stan brought a new person to the department. It was a man who was from Iran. He would be our engineer. Shirley was crushed and I was mad. Shirley had to train him for the job and it seemed so unfair. It was particularly galling because the guy didn't approve of working women and his attitude showed it.

It wasn't long before I couldn't work anymore. My rheumatologist treated me with gold shots and pain killers, which made me groggy. I went on disability and within six months of my diagnosis, I was practically bed ridden. It would sometimes take me a half hour to get out of bed. The pain was unending but I had been warned that I needed to keep moving, so I did.

The girls were attending St. Anne's Catholic School. When we moved into our house, they went to public school. One day Jo's teacher told me that she was crying every day and wouldn't go out to play. When I asked her why, she said the kids were mean and made fun of her. I went to the church and asked for help. They agreed to allow the girls to attend St. Anne's on scholarship because I didn't have the money to pay tuition. When I became ill, I could no longer drive them to school and they had to walk, even when it rained. I would watch my little girls walking down the street toward school knowing that they were cold and wet and I felt so very guilty. It hurt terribly that I couldn't do more for them.

We reached the point where the girls were doing all of the housework. I learned that I had to give up my usual standards of housekeeping; I couldn't expect them to do everything the way I would do it. I taught them to do it as well as they could for their ages. They all learned to cook and do their own laundry, too. All I could do was sit in a chair and give directions. I had to think carefully before I decided to stand up. I had to plan every step and what actions I would take. The kids learned to cook simple dishes, and I would take them to the grocery store and give them a list of what to buy. They learned to check prices and became smart shoppers. My disability pay was less than the full paycheck I had been getting, but I'd had a lot of experience in being thrifty. I'd make a calendar of menus for each day and make a shopping list from those menus. I knew exactly how much I could spend.

After a year of being on disability, the company terminated my employment. I was very disheartened because I was beginning to understand that I wasn't going to get any better and I wouldn't be able to go back to work. Since we had never received any child support from Bill, I had no choice but to apply for welfare. I was so ashamed but I couldn't let the girls go hungry. At one point, discouraged and depressed, I considered calling Bill's parents to ask them to take the girls but, in the end, I couldn't do it. I went into a severe depression, and I'm sure my girls must have suffered because of it.

When Christmas came, I was very surprised when several of my former coworkers showed up at my house. They were carrying armloads of gifts for the girls. The girls were excited and very pleased with all the presents. I felt very ambivalent—ashamed that I had to have help in providing my children's Christmas and very happy and grateful that I had such wonderful friends.

After sitting around for some months, feeling sorry for myself, I decided that I had to do something to make myself feel better. I started taking one or two classes at a time at the nearest junior college. It was very, very difficult. College campuses are notorious for their lack of parking. In the beginning, I would park and then count how many footsteps it took me to get to my class. I did my best to park as close as possible to the building where my classes were held. I also had to take into consideration whether there were any stairs to climb in the building. Each new semester, I had to take extra time to scout out where the bathrooms were, where the stairs were, and whether there were alternatives that would take fewer steps. I was in constant pain but determined to do something besides sit at home.

I discovered that I had a thirst for knowledge. Every class opened up new vistas of a world I hadn't even dreamed existed. I soaked up everything. The more I learned, the more I knew how little I had learned.

I started out just taking classes I was interested in without any clear goals. Anthropology and political science classes were the first. They fed my curiosity and my need to learn. At one point, I had to take an algebra class and I knew I wouldn't be able to concentrate because of the pain killers I was taking. My mind just couldn't stay on track. I decided I would skip the pills before class and make sure that it was the only class I had that day. The pain was distracting but I could ignore it for an hour, knowing it would end. That became my solution for taking tests as well. As hard as it was, I was at least moving forward.

One of my classes was called Comparative Religions. We discussed religions of the Near and Far East; Hinduism, Buddhism, and Shintoism were included. I was fascinated by the variety and complexities of religion in general. When we talked about Buddhism, it struck a chord. The professor explained the theory of Nirvana by saying it is believed that when you are enlightened, your soul joins the souls of those gone before and together you become one. It brought to mind the Catholic community of saints who will pray for you when asked, but it also reminded me of the Lakota belief that everyone and everything has a spirit and that we are all related. Buddhists also believe that all creatures have a soul and should not be harmed. My mind was a sponge at that time, and I felt validated that my beliefs were so common. I no longer felt abandoned by God. I didn't know where I was going with it, but it was comforting.

I plugged away at my classes and in the meantime the girls were growing up. I kept them at St. Anne's school and they did well until Terese began to notice that the kids in the public school next door seemed to be having more fun. She would hang around the fence that separated the schools, longing to be with her neighborhood friends. As they approached high school age, they all hated the school. They hated the uniforms and the fact that wearing them set them apart from everyone they knew. They disliked the nuns and the discipline they meted out. Terese began to fail and wasn't doing well when she went into high school. She was thrilled when I agreed to send her to public high school. Jo would have been happy anywhere because all she cared about was the academic part of school. Her teachers loved her because she was so smart. When she graduated from eighth grade, I took my pain medicine and made myself go to the reception. I had attended few parent-teacher meetings and certainly didn't belong to the PTA so I didn't know anyone.

A priest, the class sponsor, walked up to me and asked, "Who are you here for?"

I told him, "Jo," and he just walked away.

I decided later that I was unimportant because I wasn't one of the large contributors to the church. I thought to myself that it was odd that he neither knew nor cared why I had stopped participating in my children's schooling or church activities. I knew that the congregation regularly prayed for the sick and infirm and yet no one had ever inquired why I stopped going to Mass. We had dropped through the cracks.

Jo went on to the Catholic high school for a year and enjoyed it. Jan and Anita would go to public high school and end my career as a Catholic school mother. It also ended my spiritual life as a practicing Catholic. By then I felt that I had done what I could to ground the girls in a spiritual life and they were old enough to begin to choose their own paths.

Early in 1970 I decided I wanted to quit smoking and I read an ad for a seminar that would teach "mind control." It was a two-day seminar and I came out of it convinced that I could quit smoking and that I could do whatever I set my mind to. The method was called self-hypnosis and I learned later that it was also called, in those days, transcendental meditation. In order to communicate with our subconscious, we were told we could use meditation to quiet our conscious mind.

"Empty your mind and try to think of nothing at all."

That's what they said. It's a tall order. In order to do it, you have to concentrate on one single, simple thing that has no meaning in and of itself—a series of sounds, a candle flame, or a graphic design. It's the only way to stop thinking about yourself.

I did quit smoking and learned a lot about myself in the process. For those who don't know, meditation has nothing to do with religion or God. Prayer can be a form of meditation if you are truly engrossed in it, but meditation doesn't change your belief system. Meditation would stay with me for the rest of my life and would stand me in good stead in handling my pain.

In 1975 I finally graduated from junior college. In preparation, I talked to my counselor. He talked about my going on to get a bachelor's degree and what I would major in at the university. I really had no plans. I had been living one day at a time, just getting through.

Suddenly he asked me, "Why don't you go to law school?"

Startled, I asked, "How long would that take?"

He explained that I'd have to get a bachelor's degree and then three more years of law school. I didn't think I could do that. I was lucky to have gotten my associate's degree. I thanked him for all of his help and he wished me luck. Over the next few weeks, I thought about what he said. I was flattered that he thought I was capable of such a huge undertaking, but I wasn't sure how or if I could even manage to get a bachelor's degree.

Once I had my associate's degree, I started thinking about what I would do for the rest of my life. I knew I wanted to go to work because I just could not be a welfare mother forever. I also knew it had to be something that wasn't physical. I applied to the state vocational rehabilitation program. My counselor decided that I simply was not "college material" and needed vocational training of some kind. Court reporting looked good because I would always be sitting. In retrospect, that wasn't a good decision on my part or my counselor's part considering that my hands were affected by the arthritis. By this time, medications for the inflammation of joints had improved. Steroids were almost magical and I was able to walk within limits. The pain was never gone but it became bearable. I pushed through the pain to pound away at my court reporting machine. It didn't require strength, just stamina, and I was determined to be certified so I could get a job.

In 1977, I started looking for another house. Our neighborhood was deteriorating and becoming increasingly dangerous for my girls. An adolescent boy who lived two doors down shot another neighborhood boy.

We knew them both, and I'd watched them grow from cute little boys into rebellious youth. Poverty and parents who lacked the time and energy for them had robbed them of the life they deserved. There were simply too many opportunities for trouble in the neighborhood. The girls were shocked, and I started thinking about moving to a better neighborhood.

I have to confess now that I would occasionally do house cleaning jobs when I was desperate for money. One of the women I worked for was the wife of an attorney. She was very nice and I liked her. She came from a wealthy family and knew absolutely nothing about housekeeping. The house was beautiful, with an atrium in the middle and windows overlooking it from every side. I could wash dishes and look into the atrium and still see into the other side of the house. The master bathroom was all tile and had a shower for two with sliding glass doors leading out to a deck with a hot tub, surrounded by a privacy fence, of course. The furniture was sparse and very modern, with little evidence of the people who lived there. Even the kids' rooms were impersonal. The entire house was made of tile, glass, and gorgeous wood. It was very stiff and formal, and it wasn't a place I would have chosen to live in. I loved going there though, and the work wasn't hard because it was never really dirty and I didn't have to wash the windows.

Trudy, the lady I worked for, would talk to me while I worked. She told me about her childhood. She was an heiress without an inheritance and her family home had been turned into a museum. She had always had a nanny and there were servants to do everything so she never learned to take care of herself. Her parents inherited money but there was very little left by the time she grew up. Her husband provided for her very well, but I would sometimes hear him grousing at her for the amount of money she spent. Once they quarreled about the amount it cost for season tickets for a box at the opera.

One day Trudy began to talk to me about a seminar she went to regularly. She told me it was a self-help seminar called EST. She said it was improving her life and helping her become a better person. I couldn't imagine that her life needed improvement, but she was very enthusiastic about it. She invited me to go with her as a guest. After thinking about it, I thought it couldn't hurt so I went with her.

The seminars were the brainchild of a man named Werner Erhard. He had studied Zen Buddhism and developed the seminars to help people and to make money in the process. I found the guest seminar to be more than interesting; it touched me personally and I was surprised. It was kind of scary because I saw myself in everything the trainer said. He told us that all anybody really wants is to make a difference in this world. He also said that most of us go through life afraid of revealing our true selves because we think we're not good enough and someone might find out who we really are. That really hit home. I understood then that I had been in denial for years: trying to forget who I was and hiding out.

Still, I didn't commit myself to taking the actual seminar. I was afraid of finding out the whole truth about myself and the seminar cost $300, which I didn't have. In the meantime, I continued with my court reporter training, dreaming of the day I would pass two hundred words a minute and be able to get a job. I struggled and struggled, never noticing that my fingers were slowly but inexorably becoming deformed at the knuckles. I was just short of 200 wpm and unable to increase the speed on a regular basis.

I put my house on the market, determined to give my kids the chance to have a better life. It was a time of real estate growth in California, and I was encouraged by the realtor's promise of a sales profit that would enable me to put a large down payment on a house in a better neighborhood.

The first time I looked at our future home I was awestruck. It was a beautiful condominium with its own neighborhood. It was quiet, as mandated by the homeowners' association. The buildings were set off, apart from the rest of the neighborhood, by a low stone wall. There was a swimming pool and a tennis court, but what I liked most was the landscaping. Trees, plants, and flowers appeared in exactly the right places and gave me a sense of safety and peace. The schools were good, and I wouldn't have to worry about the girls anymore. Of course, they were teenagers and each one had her own problems, but neighbors weren't part of them.

The house itself was a one-story with three bedrooms and two baths. The kitchen and dining room were together with beautiful tile floors and counter tops. I was impressed with the window blinds, which had wooden slats. I'd never seen those before. In the living room, there was a fireplace and windows on the entire east wall, covered by soft yellow sheers that made the room seem to glow. It was all so beautiful, and I felt safe and happy. All of this was important to me because it was a symbol of how far I had come and reassured me that I was going to be okay. We all settled in for what I thought would be a long time. I kept plugging away at my court reporting, trying to keep track of my kids and dreaming of a decent future for all of us.

Eventually, I accepted a loan from Trudy so I could do "the training."

She kept urging me to go, telling me, "Take the money. You will be able to pay me back once you've had the training. Wait and see."

She was so sure something marvelous would happen to me if I took the training. It was a little scary.

The training took place on two consecutive weekends, beginning at 8 a.m. and ending whenever we were through, usually one or two o'clock in the morning. It took place in the convention center, and there were probably two hundred people in the room. We sat in hard chairs and were told there would be no bathroom breaks. There were lectures about everything we had been doing wrong with our lives and if anyone fell asleep, they would have to stand up and talk about why they were trying to avoid the subject of the lecture. I was amazed that I really didn't have to go to the bathroom when I thought I did. It was a minor thing, but what I got out of it was that my mind is in control of my body and that I was stronger than I thought. By the end of the training I could trust my brain to wake me up at a precise time and I'd be wide awake no matter how little sleep I had.

Part of the training was to get all of us to realize how little of ourselves we put into our relationships. Even those who are dearest to us seldom know our deepest secrets because we can't believe anyone would love us if they knew "the truth" about us. Bill and I had gone through ten years of marriage without ever revealing anything about our upbringing. I never told him about the racism I had suffered or even how much I adored my brothers. He never told me anything about his family or why he ran away at sixteen years old, joined the army, and never really went home again. Eventually, his sisters would tell me what little they knew about him. Neither of us trusted that the other would stick around knowing who we really were.

During the training, in pursuit of being able to open up to other people, we practiced on the strangers around us.

"Tell the person next to you about a time when you were happy," the trainer would say.

Oh, my gosh! Talking to strangers was really hard for me. My cultural upbringing had always led me to be quiet and keep a low profile when I was alone among strangers. Be careful until you know the lay of the land. That was the way I operated. Here I was, in a room full of strangers who were mostly white people. I didn't want to embarrass myself, so I did what they asked (within limits). Besides, I had paid a lot of money to be there.

I was surprised when the trainer told us to close our eyes as he began to lead us through the process of meditation. The method was different from anything I had learned before but the results were the same. He sent us on many and various imaginary trips. We built an imaginary house where we felt safe and loved and climbed a giant flower. That's about all I can tell you about the physical part of the training, the things we actually did. I do recall that there were some exercises where we had to stand for long periods. My knees hurt so badly, but I was too embarrassed to ask to sit down. I didn't want to draw attention to myself so I pushed through the pain and stuck it out. I really don't remember much else. I just remember how I felt afterwards.

The crux of the training was to get us to understand: *"You and I possess, at every moment of our lives, under all circumstances, the power to transform the quality of our lives."* (Werner Erhard)

One of the trainer's exhortations that stuck in my mind forever was, "Take responsibility for your life!"

I got it! Whatever had happened in my life before was done. I could change my future, but only by taking my life in my own hands. I couldn't sit around anymore and wait to see what life would bring. I had to make it happen!

My mother had been living in Sacramento with Deed since 1974. After Dad died, she lived alone until she developed congestive heart failure. We were all worried because she lived so far from good health care. Eventually and against her better judgment, she sold all of her household goods and moved to California. She tried to adjust, but she was never really happy.

Deed helped her plant a small garden, but when the tomato plants grew to four feet tall and she found four-inch worms on them, she complained, "I hate California. Everything is too big here!"

Deed would come home from work to find her scrubbing the already clean kitchen floor on her hands and knees. She was trying to find something to make her feel useful. In 1978, after several bouts with congestive heart failure, she began to weaken appreciably. She became unhappy with her living situation and decided to live with Teewee for a while. She also stayed with me for a few months. I watched her become weaker as her heart deteriorated. She never complained, but soon it was all she could do to eat her meals and go to the bathroom. At first, she tried to crochet as she had done for most of her life. She was working on a throw rug for me. The rug was to be used in front of the couch and was made from heavy yarn. Soon she became so weak she could no longer lift it and she had to give up. My heart ached because I knew I was losing her.

Mom was a tiny little woman, quiet but strong. I don't ever remember her yelling at me or any of the kids.

Scolding consisted of her saying, "My girl, you shouldn't do that."

Being a farm wife was not her dream job, to say the least. It was sheer unrelenting drudgery and hard work, but she never complained or reduced her expectations of herself or us. She accepted her lot and made the best of it. She was rarely, if ever, in bad humor. One of my memories of her is standing at the dining room table, forming loaves of bread and biscuits and singing.

I seldom heard my parents argue. If they disagreed, it was done quietly. For the most part, Mom didn't argue with Dad. If it was something she really wanted to do, she simply went ahead and did it. I only remember one occasion when a disagreement was so serious as to affect the family. Mom was offered a job in Rapid City. Dad didn't want her to go, but we needed the money. Dad was so upset that he must have threatened divorce or separation because Mom wanted me to go with her. She even offered a bribe—a beautiful cedar keepsake box. As much as I wanted the box, I didn't want to leave home. Eventually, she gave in and didn't go, but she gave me the box anyway.

Mom lived her Christian values. She was gentle, soft spoken, and unfailingly kind. She worried about the elders in the community. She gave them vegetables from our garden, and in the winter she would urge the men in the family to cut and haul wood for them. She loved her church and did everything she could for the priest and the church. She cleaned the church and the priest's house. She would wash, starch, and iron the priest's surplices and the scarves that covered the altar. She gathered secondhand clothing and sorted and washed them for rummage sales for the church. If the clothing was not wearable, she cut off buttons and zippers and saved them. She would then determine whether or not to cut the clothing up to be used for quilting. I was a frequent helper in this enterprise.

Death did not come easily to Mom. After one last bout of congestive heart failure, she didn't bounce back. She lay in her bed in Teewee's house and slowly faded. Her heart was weak and her kidneys began to fail. She was in great pain, and when I asked her if she wanted me to read from her Bible, she accepted. She knew she was dying and accepted it as she had accepted all the hardships in her life. I kissed her goodnight, knowing I might not see her in the morning. She urged me to go home and get some sleep—Mother to the end.

It was September 1979 and I was still plugging away at my court reporting. My daughter Jo had graduated from high school and started college classes. She and I were at odds because she had decided she wanted to become a Mormon. I was not happy. It felt like a betrayal and I tried desperately to change her mind, reminding her that the Mormons had a huge role in trying to destroy our culture by removing Indian children from their homes and families and teaching them that our beliefs were bad and wrong. It brought back too many memories of boarding school and racism. She was eighteen and simply loved the social life she found with the Mormons, among other things. Nothing I said had any effect, and we did our best to live with the differences of opinion. One day, I was talking to one of her church "elders" about Jo and he asked me about my schooling. For some reason, I told him about my counselor's advice that I should go to law school, and that I felt it would take too long because I was too old.

He then said the words that would change my life.

"What would you be doing in five years anyway?" he asked.

What would I be doing? The question caused me to stop and take a look at what my life was about right then. I was just surviving. It wasn't a bad life, really. Two of my girls had pretty much dropped out of regular school and had gone on to alternative school. By then, through the knowledge gained at the EST training, I had accepted the fact that they were going to make their own decisions about their lives. I had learned the lesson that all parents must eventually learn: children have to make their own mistakes in order to grow. It's a difficult lesson, and it caused me many sleepless nights and a lot of crying. In looking at what my life was about, I decided that it mattered very little what I was doing.

My children would keep doing whatever they were doing. Surely, I had the right to have a life of my own. I worried that one day my disease would make it impossible for me to take care of myself. Without more education, I could become a burden on my children. Having come to that conclusion, I was free to make decisions about what to do with my own life. What would I be doing in five years? The girls would be out of school and I'd be on my own anyway, so why not do something I really wanted to do? I began thinking about law school.

As soon as I started thinking seriously about law school, I thought about my brother Bob. He was a very unique person. I had never been very close to him because he simply never had time for me or my sisters. He was always driven by his passions. I admired him tremendously and I knew that Dad thought the sun rose and set in him. When he was a little boy in Rosebud, he would trudge the dusty streets and roads of the community, looking for pop bottles that he could redeem for spending money. Resourceful and independent, he was ever conscious of the responsibilities imposed on him by Lakota culture. Like Dad, he believed in Lakota spirituality and sought out the advice of medicine men. When he came home from the war, he decided that he needed to have a voice in tribal government. He began by running for and winning a seat on the tribal council. At age twenty-eight, he became tribal chairman, which he would repeat for four more terms. He was a politician and loved being a leader. In 1961, he resigned as president of the tribe and became president of the National Congress of American Indians.[1] Influenced by his Lakota upbringing, he was a leader with a heart. He did everything he could to help the needy and especially, the elders.

Years later, at his funeral, I heard an old woman cry, "Who's going to take care of us now?"

He was always conscious that Indian people were being denied their civil rights on nearly a daily basis. He became an advocate for Indian civil rights. He would take it upon himself to make sure that civil rights issues were brought to the attention of federal officials.

In 1971 he wrote a book titled *The Tortured Americans*, decrying the problems of tribal government that he wanted changed.[2] He wrote a second book in 1974, coauthored by John Koster, *The Road to Wounded Knee*, in which he chronicled the history of the federal government's continuing failure to keep its promises.[3]

Even when he was not in office, he continued to do whatever he could to ensure that the government of the Rosebud Sioux Tribe was honest and that the welfare of the people was foremost in the minds of the tribal government. To that end, when he felt it was necessary, he would draft legal documents to file in court. In those days, the tribe didn't have the money to hire attorneys. Bob would go on the road to raise money for his causes. He became fast friends with Doris Duke, who so believed in him and his work that she donated enough money for the tribe to be able to buy a herd of cattle and other necessities. He would raise the money, draft the documents, and hire an attorney to present them in court. I called him one day to suggest that if I went to law school, we could work together. I would be there to serve as his attorney and together we could do more for the people.

He said, "Sure," but he wasn't so sure I could get into law school.

It was September 1979 when my precious Mom kissed me good night and passed on from this life. I kept moving through my own life, but it was a façade. Pain came in unexpected waves and left me in tears at inconvenient times and places. I kept trying to manage my teenagers and continued with my court reporting classes, but nothing was the same.

One day, on the bus going home from class, I started to think about Mom and cry. The thought came to me that now I had become my children's link to the past. What past? The one I had been ignoring and running from for twenty years? I was forty years old and I didn't really know who I was as an adult. Right then I felt that all I could do was to keep moving forward. I could do more with my life than I had done before.

Twelve

A PARADIGM SHIFT

With Mom gone, there was nothing to hold me in Sacramento. I knew that my limits were set only by what I thought I could do. The idea of law school had, at first, seemed really far-fetched. I had never dreamed such dreams. The fact that my brother Bob could do such things pushed me to believe it was possible. I knew I wanted to do something worthwhile and going home to the reservation could be it.

I began thinking about what it would take for me to be able to go to law school. First of all, I would have to complete a bachelor's degree. I would have to pass the Law School Admission Test and find the money for law school, but first I had to decide which school(s) I would apply to.

I knew by then that I had to go to a school that specialized in Federal Indian Law. I knew from my research, living on the reservation and listening to Dad and Bob talk, that we (Indians) were a special people and that some laws were different for us. The University of New Mexico looked perfect. They had the best Indian Law program in the country and, thanks to the American Indian Law Center, scholarships were available.

Once I made the decision to go to UNM law school, the other decisions were easy. The thought of moving to Albuquerque was a little scary. I had never been to the southwest and, although I had a niece who lived there, I would essentially be leaving my family behind. When I told them what I was going to do, they were astounded. Johnny warned me against selling my condominium. He felt that owning a house was a hedge against the future and that I would regret it. A home of your own was, after all, the American dream and we should pass it on to our kids. Teewee and Deed thought I was crazy because I had no guarantee that I would be able to carry out my plans.

I had absolutely no second thoughts. I knew that my intentions were enough to create success. I put the condo on the market with the goal of leaving for Albuquerque by the first of August (1980) so I could register for classes to finish my bachelor's degree.

I told the girls and asked them to decide whether they wanted to go with me. Jo was nineteen and in college. She had met someone and decided that she would get married. Although I felt she was too young, she was old enough to make her own decisions. She and Neil had extraordinary communications and I thought they could make a go of it, so I gave my blessing. Neil always made me laugh.

When Jo introduced us, he shook my hand and asked, "And how long have you known Jo?"

Thirty-three years later, they are still married, and he can still make me laugh with his lame jokes.

Terese had already left home and was living on her own. I wasn't sure Jan was ready to be on her own, but she was in a rebellious state and refused to go with me. Anita was only sixteen and I didn't give her a choice. She wasn't happy about moving and changing schools, but she would go with me.

On moving day, I had a U-Haul truck loaded and drove around completing last-minute errands. I had to leave my old station wagon behind with Jo. It was in such disrepair that I knew it wouldn't have made it to Albuquerque. I drove to the office of my vocational rehabilitation counselor to turn in my court reporting machine. I'll never forget the look on his face when I told him I was going to Albuquerque to go to law school. I'm sure he thought I was crazy, too. After all, I wasn't "college material."

Anita, me, and our dog, Ginger, drove to the real estate office, picked up a check for the sale proceeds and headed for a new life. Two days later we arrived at the outskirts of Albuquerque at two o'clock in the morning. We'd had difficulty finding motels that would take Ginger, and I was very sleepy. We stopped at one of the first motels we came to and didn't look around very much. It was fairly clean and very quiet at that time of night. We didn't mention Ginger and she spent the night with us. The next morning, in daylight, everything looked different. There were glaring neon signs everywhere up and down the road, signs that called to a different clientele. In my drowsy state, I had missed the fact that we were stopping in the "red light district." We left in a hurry.

That day we got our first real look at our new home. I thought it was beautiful. With the Sangre de Cristo Mountains in the background, the city flowed down toward the Rio Grande. I loved the adobe houses with their xeriscape yards; they all looked so clean and crisp. Later on, as we became more familiar with New Mexico, I found tremendous beauty in the rugged landscape colored in vibrant reds and oranges. Somehow, perhaps it was God's presence, there was peace there. Anita wasn't so thrilled and complained about the constant singing of the cicadas. She missed California's trees and flowers and most of all, she missed her friends. I realized she was homesick and tried to distract her with helping me find a house and buy a car.

There were constant logistical problems but we managed to get through them. Finding an apartment was difficult because few managers would accept a dog. Eventually, we settled on a brand-new apartment in the far reaches of the foothills above the city.

When we found a car we wanted, it was a stick shift and neither of us knew how to drive it. It turned out to be fun as the seller bravely set out to teach us. He convinced me that I would soon conquer the jerks I produced at every start. Anita and I laughed a lot that day, as we learned to drive that car. Everything worked out perfectly, and we were ready for our new life.

As we settled in, I had an old debt to settle. I sent Trudy a check for $300 for the loan she'd given me to go to the "training." The money debt was paid, but I will be forever grateful to her for insisting that I go.

In order to stretch my money, I found a part-time job as a secretary/ receptionist for a construction company. I registered as a full-time student at the University of New Mexico, majoring in elementary education. I reasoned that if I didn't get into law school, I could always teach.

Anita enrolled as a high school junior. Within a short time, Jan was in dire straits and I sent her money to join us. It was a relief because I had felt so guilty for leaving her even though I knew she had to make her own decisions. In the meantime, Jo and Neil got married and settled in Sacramento. My family was adjusting to a new phase in our lives, one that I hoped would better all of our lives.

Within weeks, I changed my priorities. I became a full-time student with a self-imposed deadline of two years. UNM was a huge campus, and I was intimidated and overwhelmed. There were so many activities, and I wanted to take part in everything. I was thrilled to be there even though I still had to plan my parking and count my steps to class.

As part of my teacher training, I became a tutor for Indian kids. My first student was a little Pueblo boy who was struggling with reading. As we worked on his reading, he told me that he was an Indian but he didn't know "what kind." He had been adopted by a white couple and they wanted him to know about his culture.

I talked to my niece who was married to a man from Laguna Pueblo. They agreed to introduce my little student to Pueblo ceremonies. It was an unforgettable day. The ceremonies were beautiful and awe inspiring. The masked dancers were attentive to the little boy and presented him with several gifts. I could tell he was scared but he never flinched. I was touched by the thought that the little boy might never have known about them but for us.

Sitting there, steeped in a centuries-old ceremony, I envied the child his opportunity to learn about his culture. My thoughts turned toward home. I realized that I knew very little about my own culture, besides going to powwows.

The summer of 1981, I decided to go home. I didn't know when I would get another chance once I started law school. Mom and Dad were gone and I knew everything had changed. I called my little brother, Jim, to ask if I could stay with him and his family.

Jim and Lydia had been married for twenty years and had five children. They had gone to California for a time, on the Relocation Program, but had decided that they didn't want to live the city life and returned to the reservation.

Jim had been participating in powwow dancing for quite a while. He loved to dance and would participate whether or not he had his regalia with him. He had learned so much about our culture from Lydia, who spoke Lakota and had been raised in a traditional home. They both became part of the American Indian Movement in the '70s and participated in the struggle at Wounded Knee in 1973.[1]

I admired them both, and spending time with them made me realize how much I missed home and family. It was wonderful to go to Rosebud

Fair again and to watch the familiar dances. I loved spending time with my baby nieces. One night, as we laid in bed, they started talking about spirits. Suddenly one of them decided she'd seen one and they ran and jumped into bed with me. We giggled and laughed until we fell asleep.

When I went back to Albuquerque, it was time to think about law school. I knew I had to take the Law School Admission Test (LSAT), and I had no idea how to study for it. I didn't know anyone who had or would be taking the test, so I was on my own. I soon learned that there were practice tests available, and they made me nervous. In those days, the test even included math. It was pretty nerve-racking. The pamphlet said to take a quarter, a candy bar, and a watch. The candy bar was to keep up your energy (it was a long test), the watch was for you to make sure you were answering at a steady pace, and the quarter was for tossing when you didn't know the answer. I walked out without the foggiest idea of how I would come out.

By the time I took the test, I had decided that I was going to law school, no matter what. If my test scores were poor, I would try again. If I didn't get accepted to UNM Law School, I would re-apply. I knew that there were about 700 applicants every year and only 100 would be accepted. I had increased my chances for acceptance by moving to New Mexico and becoming a resident of the state. So, having done everything I could to ensure my success, I wrote the essay for my application and sent it in with a prayer.

As I began my last year of undergraduate work, my money was running out. We took Ginger to California to live with my niece and found a cheaper place to live.

In October, my life became more complicated when I suddenly became the caretaker for my baby granddaughter. Fortunately, Jan and Anita were happy to help. I could never have taken on such responsibility without them. I was anxious because I knew I had to find the money for law school, and everyone said that it was impossible to work and do the required studying as a first-year law student.

I began to have panic attacks although it wasn't called that in those days. With my heart racing and my breathing increased, I would get dizzy and light-headed. I was sure I was going to pass out and die. Fear was the worst thing. I had to overcome it to stop the attack. The doctor prescribed a brown paper bag. He told me to breathe into it to increase my carbon dioxide level. And once more, my meditation practice came through for me. It helped me overcome the fear and increased anxiety and, after a couple of months, the attacks stopped.

One evening in November, I got a phone call from Jim. He was depressed because he couldn't find a job. We talked about his coming to New Mexico to work in the oil fields and he talked about his kids. A few nights later I got another phone call, and I can't remember who it was who told me Jim had died. I couldn't believe it. He was just forty years old. He'd had a massive heart attack. My niece and I drove the 900 miles back to the reservation. My family was in turmoil. Everyone was in shock. Jim was the baby of the family, and he wasn't supposed to die first. My sisters were positive that his death was caused by something other than natural causes. They wanted to blame someone for it and demanded an autopsy. I could only think about Lydia and the kids.

I remembered how much he loved them all and the way he had carried the smallest girl to her kindergarten class when she cried. He adored his children and Lydia. When he and Lydia quarreled, he had warned me not to take sides. We buried his ashes, at his request, partly on a hill overlooking our old homeplace at Two Kettle and partly in the family plot.

My heart ached as I returned to New Mexico and my classes. I had to ask for counseling and extra help with my studies. I couldn't concentrate, and my grief was overwhelming. I had lost my beloved playmate. It was too late to go back and get to know him better as an adult, but I did know he was a kind, loving person.

My last semester included student teaching in a second-grade classroom. It was great fun and I really loved the kids. The rest of my life was hectic with classes and family matters. I put in an application to attend UNM's Pre-Law Summer Institute. PLSI is a short, trial version of the first-year of law school for Indian students. I wasn't accepted, and I was terribly disappointed because it would have given me a chance to become familiar with law school. The denial made me nervous and I wondered if it meant I wouldn't be accepted to UNM Law.

One day, after work, Jan came into the apartment with the mail. She had a smile on her face and looked excited.

She said, "Mom, you got a letter from UNM."

I caught my breath and told her to open it. I just couldn't do it myself.

She opened the envelope and started to read, "We are pleased to inform you . . ." or some such language.

Then we were both yelling and hugging each other. I couldn't believe it! I actually got in on the first round! Law school admissions are done in stages or rounds. In other words, students are selected in batches as the Admissions Committee builds the class they want. I felt honored that they had chosen me so quickly. I didn't go to my bachelor's degree graduation because it felt anticlimactic. I quit my job and we made a trip to California to visit the family.

Thirteen

LAW SCHOOL

August 1983: Law school orientation. I hadn't dared to check out the building before. I still didn't feel like I belonged there, not even after all my determination to be there. I walked into the wide expanse of the forum, with its dark wood paneling cut with a wall of glass doors leading outside. The high ceiling sheltered the area with its scattering of groups of chairs here and there. I felt small and very alone. Groups of first-year students stood around, waiting to see what was going to happen. It was a diverse group—Hispanics, Indians, whites, a smattering of Asians, and one African American.

Several women sat behind tables with papers and small file boxes in front of them. We were asked to form several lines in front of the seated women according to the first letter of our last names. It became obvious that as you came to the front of the line, the woman would search her file box for your name and pull a card from the box.

As I stood in line, I thought to myself, "Oh, my gosh. I'm going to get up there and she's going to tell me there's been a mistake and my name isn't there."

I held my breath until she pulled the card out and verified the spelling of my name. I was in!

We were then taken on a tour of the school, introduced to some staff and faculty, and given a blow-by-blow description of what we could expect. I'd never heard of the Socratic method of teaching, and I didn't have the foggiest notion what it meant. More or less, it means teaching by asking questions. The classrooms were large and intimidating. Built on a sloping floor, they gave the professor a clear view of every student, wherever they sat.

I'd always loved books and libraries, but the law library scared me. I was awestricken. It was the biggest library I'd ever seen, and my confusion was heightened by the librarian who gave us a guided tour. I didn't know what she was talking about. I didn't know how I was ever going to learn what books were where.

One of the first classes we had was a research class to teach us how to find the books we would need to research a legal case. We were given a specific case and questions about it. We had to find the right books to get the answers, and we were introduced to the politics of law school. Some person or persons got their answers and then hid some of the books to prevent the rest of us from being able to finish the assignment on time. It was propelled by the rush to be sure they would be at the top of the class. Class ranking was of the utmost importance if they hoped to be hired by a large law firm. They would trade their integrity for a top ranking. I and others were frantic when we couldn't find the books, and I assumed I was looking in the wrong places and just couldn't find them. Later on, someone figured it out and eventually we all knew we were in for some heavy-duty competition. As old as I was, I was pretty naïve and it was the beginning of my education in the realities of the white man's legal world.

The first year of law school is traditionally horrific. We were given so many reading assignments it was impossible to get them done. The vocabulary was all new (to some of us), and my reading comprehension was low as I struggled to understand the complexity of legal arguments.

To add to the difficulty, those were the days before computers and I typed all my papers on a tiny portable typewriter. I remember well staying up all night to type a paper in Criminal Law. The question we had to answer proved to be rather circular and I typed several different versions. To make sense of it, I ended up cutting it into paragraphs and physically rearranging them to flow properly. I had to tape the individual paragraphs to a single sheet and copy it so it appeared to have been typed on the page. It was an all-nighter.

Many of my classmates had an easier time because they'd had at least a passing acquaintance with legalese. They either came from families with lawyers or had worked in the legal world. Sometimes I had to read the same thing over and over. It became normal to read until one or two o'clock in the morning every night. I learned to take quick naps. Between classes, I'd go to the library, put my head on my arm, and sleep for ten minutes to get me through the day. I was tired all the time.

The school's Socratic method of teaching traumatized me every day. I'd walk into the classroom and try to find a seat that would allow me to be as invisible as possible. The professor would throw out a question and then pin down a hapless student to dare to answer. There would ensue, hopefully, an argument from someone else and we'd all learn something.

I didn't see it that way though. What I saw was someone giving a wrong answer and being humiliated for his ignorance. You have to understand that public humiliation is a no-no in Lakota culture. You wouldn't do that to your worst enemy. You have to allow everyone to maintain their self-respect. Respect others and they will respect you. I had never realized how deeply that mantra was ingrained in me. That precept had been violated over and over again in my life. It began in boarding school with pubic whippings and continued with my own husband treating me with scorn.

Law school became a continuation of all the oppression I had suffered. It became my deepest dread every day. There were, I think, about nine Indian students who began first year and I believe only three of us graduated. I wonder now how many of them were as intimidated as I was and unable to adjust.

I never told anyone at school about the rheumatoid arthritis. I was fortunate to have a wonderful doctor at the Indian Health facility. The pain dogged my every step, and I thanked God the law school wasn't spread out. The stress and lack of sleep exacerbated the disease, and my joints often swelled from the inflammation. I took pain medication when I felt the need, but I avoided it as much as possible.

The only thing that kept me going was my determination and the fact that I had such wonderful classmates. I had some difficulty fitting in with the rest of the Indian students because I was so much older than they and most of them had bonded in the Summer Institute sessions. There was one other woman who was about my age. Her name was Rachel and she was Mexican American. Soon we were pals and went everywhere together. Because we both had dark hair, the professors would sometimes mix us up. She was better than I in assimilating into the social world of law school. The younger Mexican American students accepted both of us, and we were invited to parties and other social gatherings, which also contributed to our education. At every event, there were discussions of law and politics. I loved it and it assured me that I really was learning something even though it didn't feel that way when I was in class.

Midway in the first semester I got a chance to go to New Orleans to attend the National Indian Education Association conference. It was exciting and my first chance to stay in a big hotel. At the very first plenary session, I looked across the room and there was my brother Bob. I couldn't believe my eyes. It was the first time we'd met since Jim's death. I walked over to him and we greeted one another like acquaintances. It was obvious that the old pain hadn't passed.

Later that day, I went on a walking tour of New Orleans. I walked down Bourbon Street and peeked into little souvenir shops and bistros blaring music. I watched people hanging from balconies, shouting to others in the street while young boys danced for money. I walked around Jackson Square and then hailed a cab to look for a place to eat. The cabbie took me to a small restaurant where I had the best gumbo ever.

Later that evening, I got sick. I developed a severe pain in my chest. I lay on the bed and waited for it to go away. After a while, I got scared. I thought I might be having a heart attack. I didn't know what to do so I called my brother. He came right away and took me to the local ER. The ER was horrible. Crowded with people crying and yelling, it smelled of sweat and urine. The line for triage was long and wound into the hallway. We waited a bit and made small talk. I told him about my afternoon and the gumbo. Soon we decided that the ER was too much and maybe I just had indigestion. We went back to the hotel, and he bought me some antacid. We went to our separate rooms, never realizing that we would never see each other again. The pain of Jim's death was passed over and smoothed out.

First year passed and during the summer I was asked to be a tutor for the incoming Pre-Law Summer Institute students. In the process, I learned as much as the new students. Some of them would become UNM students and some would go on to Ivy League schools. They were a great bunch and I liked them all.

During my second year, things began to gel for me. I signed up to work in the free legal clinic to help low-income people with legal problems. Mostly, I did investigations, trying to put the cases together. It was interesting, and I loved working with the clients.

One day, one of my classmates asked if I wanted to join an organization to help battered women. I agreed, even though I wasn't sure what we'd be doing. As it turned out, school and studying limited what I could do, but joining the organization opened my eyes and I learned more about myself than I ever dreamed.

As part of the orientation, we volunteers were given information about domestic violence and its effects. I had never thought of myself as a battered woman. True to form, I had thought our arguing and fighting were just part of marriage and I had kept hoping it was going to change if I just did everything right. It never occurred to me that the violent behavior was illegal and should never have happened.

I sat in amazement as the group facilitator enumerated all of the signs of an abusive relationship and I recognized them all. I had been physically assaulted, isolated from friends and family, and emotionally and financially controlled. I knew then that the different forms of abuse had come on so gradually and insidiously that I had never realized that they were increasing in frequency and intensity. Over time, it was so pervasive that it would only take a threat, a few harsh words, or a look to convince me that I was about to be assaulted again. I had lived under a constant cloud of fear.

When I discovered that women typically stay in a battering relationship and try to change it, I began to understand that I wasn't as weak or stupid as I'd been feeling. I was astounded that so many women were caught in the same situation and couldn't get out. I began to recover some of my self-esteem, but I was still too ashamed to admit to anyone that I had been a battered woman.

In September 1984, I was working in the legal clinic when I got a phone call from my niece. No one ever called me at school, so it was startling. She told me that my brother Bob had died in his sleep. I had just seen him in New Orleans; it was less than two years after Jim's death and I was shocked. We packed our bags and drove home to the reservation.

I don't remember very much about the funeral except that there were so many people it had to be held in a gymnasium. Activist that he was, he was always controversial. He'd had several threats on his life and the FBI insisted on an autopsy to settle the issue of his cause of death. He'd had a heart attack at forty-nine, which left his heart damaged and he had a pacemaker. The autopsy showed that he'd had a massive heart attack.

Our family had become divided when Jim died, and I felt like Bob's death was a continuation of Jim's. The worst part for me was a feeling of abandonment. I hadn't realized how much I had been counting on Bob to be there when I finished school. It was in my mind that we were going to work together. I was going to be his lawyer and we'd do great things. I went back to school with a feeling of emptiness. I would have to re-set my goals.

The deaths of my brothers and the trips back to the reservation had reawakened my connections to home. I belonged to the Native American Law Students Association and when we met everyone talked about their home reservations and all the legal problems the tribes had with the federal government and the states.

I thought of all the things I could do, but most of the time I just thought about going home. I could help the tribe, but most of all, I could help the people. Although I didn't feel worthy, maybe I could still fulfill Bob's legacy.

During that year, I began to be aware of the impact the white man's law had had on my own life. I sat in Property Law and Criminal Law classes and wondered how anyone could have come to the conclusion that someone's property could be worth a human life. It didn't make sense to me. It amazed me that you could shoot someone to protect yourself, your family, or your property. It just didn't fit in with anything I knew or felt. It bothered me, and I found myself wondering why it didn't seem to bother anyone else. It was all about land and property. What happened to justice?

In the meantime, I was also taking a class in Federal Indian Law. The best part of the class was learning the legal history of our tribes. There was so much I didn't know. I had accepted my life on the reservation and never wondered why it was so. Now I knew, and it was painful. Once again, it was all about land.

I learned about the Indian Removal Act, which was behind the tragic story of the forced removal of the Cherokee, Choctaw, Muscogee, Seminole, and Chickasaw tribes.[1] It's known as The Trail of Tears, and the people didn't just cry because they had to leave their homeland. Thousands of people died in the process, of starvation and exposure. Imagine walking from the East Coast to Oklahoma! I had to look up The Trail of Tears because the subject of the class was the legalities leading up to the removal. The class didn't delve into the details of what happened to the people and how they must have felt. It was really heartbreaking to learn the extent to which the American government went to obtain Indian land, and it was only the beginning.

For Sioux people, each individual having been given land by the Dawes Act didn't mean very much. We had no concept of land ownership, having had complete use of the entire prairie. The land grab began with the Fort Laramie Treaty of 1851, when the government established boundaries between some tribes. That was only the beginning. Next came the Fort Laramie Treaty of 1868 and we ceded more of our land to establish the Great Sioux Reservation. Our world was closing in on us. Then came the Agreement with the Sioux of 1889, which established separate reservations and further restricted our movements. The Dawes Act would prove to be the federal government's solution to getting everything they wanted from us: our land and our way of life.

At first we weren't even considered to be citizens. Then, in order to get us to be farmers and to become literate, they gave us citizenship and title to our individual allotments as a reward. We were said to have become "competent Indians" and we could sell our own land.

By the time I was born in 1938, many Indian people had sold the land they received as allotments, including my parents. Even though Indians had been educated to a certain extent, they were by no means wise to the ways of the white man. I was told by one of our elders that it was common practice for white men to stand at the doors of the BIA to find out about Indians who died so they could approach the heirs to buy their newly inherited land. They were consolidating their holdings and we were, for the most part, oblivious that it was important to do so.

As I learned the legal story of Indian tribes, I began to understand some of what had happened to me and my family. A window opened and I could see and feel the oppression and racism that had inundated us from the very beginning. My heart began to ache. I knew we were in the throes of trying to take care of ourselves within the restrictions placed on us by the federal government.

Worst of all, I began to see the federal government as the enemy and white people as their agents. I thought about Mom's and Dad's struggles, and Bob's yearning for a better tribal government and better lives for our people. I lost my self-confidence and wondered why I ever thought that I could make a difference. It all seemed too big and overwhelming. I went through a period of depression, and it became difficult to make myself go to classes.

I couldn't quit and let it go. I had committed myself to reach a goal and graduation was only part of it. I had to find a way to reconcile what I was learning and what I was feeling.

Final exams took a toll on me. One of the professors gave us a take-home exam. It was an essay, to be written in a specified amount of time. In law school, a great deal of emphasis was put on "honor." In this instance, we were on our honor to complete the exam within the required time. I started to write, and about midway I developed pain in my chest. I tried desperately to continue but soon I was doubled over with the pain. I had to call the school to let them know I couldn't continue the exam. I went to the emergency room only to be told that they could find no reason for the pain. I found out later that it was an esophageal spasm brought on by stress. In fact, after a couple of hours it began to diminish and I called to tell my professor I would resume the exam. He told me I wouldn't get a grade, just a pass/fail. I was disappointed to lose the opportunity to improve my grade point average, but I understood that it was their assurance that students would gain nothing by cheating. I remembered my first week of school and the hidden books and I knew why they had to do it.

I used part of the semester break to fly to California to visit my sisters. I told Teewee that I felt like I had been wounded and turned inside out. Anxiety and depression rolled over me and only the presence of my family helped me keep my head up. They grounded me and reminded me of my original dream of working with Bob to make things better at home. After that, I often referred to law school as boot camp because they had, to a certain extent, torn me apart and I had to put myself back together. I would never be the same, but I would be stronger.

I slept ten hours my first night "home." I felt safe in the arms of my family. We talked about home and family, and I remembered all the things I had loved growing up. I began to feel better.

In the days that followed, I finally came to terms with my dilemma. I decided that I needed to adopt the philosophy that law school was an opportunity to "know thine enemy" and that I didn't have to agree with everything they were trying to teach.[2] I needed to find my own niche and stop trying to change my way of thinking. I hugged my sisters and went back to Albuquerque.

Second year, second semester went by uneventfully until the last week. We had begun final exams again and it was the first morning. The first exam I had was Criminal Law. I was getting dressed when the telephone rang. I was in a rush because we didn't dare be late or we would be excluded from the exam. I picked up the phone and heard a woman's voice announcing that she was a nurse in the emergency room of a hospital in Reno, Nevada. I was stunned to hear that she was with my daughter Terese. She said that Terese had been in a car accident and was severely injured. She had no other information because Terese was on her way to the operating room.

She told me that Terese was basically incoherent, but she kept repeating my phone number and saying, "Call my mom."

I took down the phone number at the hospital and, in a state of shock, finished dressing and hurried off to my exam.

Once seated in the classroom with my exam papers, I told myself not to think about Terese because the hospital would have no further information until the operation was finished and I might as well get on with my exam. It proved to be a futile effort. I started reading the exam questions and realized that practically everything I had read over the last few days was gone out of my mind. I couldn't concentrate, and I couldn't make heads or tails of once familiar legal cases. I tried to struggle my way through it, but once the allotted time was finished I knew that I had failed. I went home and broke down and cried, both for my daughter and my failed exam. I found out later that I didn't fail but it wasn't a good grade either. I didn't have time to worry about it.

I called the hospital and was told that Terese had a shattered pelvis and that they were trying to save her right leg. I knew that I had to be with her. I called my advisor at the school and explained to her what had happened. She told me that I should not have attempted the exam and that I shouldn't take any more. She advised me to leave immediately to be with Terese. She explained to me that I could take the rest of my exams when I returned to school in the fall.

I took my little granddaughter, Erika, who was Terese's daughter, and drove to Reno as fast as I could. I went immediately to the intensive care unit where Terese lay sedated and with her leg encased in a metal contraption. The doctor informed me that all of her calf muscles had been stripped from the bone and her main artery in that area had been torn. He said they were trying to piece together the artery but it didn't look promising. He asked me whether I thought she would want them to do everything possible to save her leg. The muscles were so torn that she would never again be able to bend her knee or ankle. I looked at her legs and feet. They had been so beautiful and she was always proud of them. I thought to myself that she would not want an ugly leg. As it turned out, I didn't have to make the decision because the artery proved to be too badly shredded and they couldn't save her leg.

Once her leg was amputated, she left the intensive care unit and was moved to the rehabilitation unit. We were told that it would be several weeks before she could leave the hospital. I decided to stay in Reno to be with her for as long as necessary. That meant that I would have to find a job and a place to live. I found a room with a kitchenette in a cute old house owned by a very tiny, very old lady. I found daycare for Erika and started job hunting.

As it happened, my niece, Rae, was living and working in Reno. She helped me find a job. It was an internship at the offices of Nevada Legal Services in Sparks. I was thrilled when I actually got the job and I was introduced to the world of poverty law. Up to that point, I didn't know there was such a thing.

The Legal Services Corporation (LSC) is a nonprofit corporation established in 1974. It reflected the antipoverty culture of the time. It was established to promote equal access to justice and provides funds to serve poor people. Nevada Legal Services was just one of many programs under LSC. I soon discovered that LSC funded legal services on many Indian reservations and I began to think that Legal Services might be a good choice for me.

We spent the entire summer supporting Terese as she went through a very painful healing process and adjusting to being without her leg. August came and Terese was well enough to travel. Erika and I drove back to Albuquerque and Teewee helped Terese get on a plane. The next year would be a difficult one for her.

Third year began with my having to finish my second-year final exams. Because they were taken out of time, they would all be graded on a pass/fail basis. Disappointment rolled over me as I realized that two semesters wouldn't be enough to pull up my GPA to be able to compete for the "best" jobs. My ego really wanted to be able to say that I was that good.

Up to that point, I knew I wanted to go home, but I wasn't sure how. I had set my sights on civil rights work with Bob. Now I just didn't know how I could get into it.

Starting classes, I was a little more confident because I had some work experience under my belt and I would do the best I could in this, my last year. Everyone was talking about jobs, and I couldn't see myself in any of them. I knew I wanted to work with people, and I loved my Negotiation and Mediation class. I began to consider what I might actually want to do.

The end of classes and finals and I still wasn't sure what I could or wanted to do. And then came graduation. We gathered at the law school for our hooding ceremony. That's a ceremony of special recognition for someone getting a doctoral degree. My entire family had gathered. They came from California by plane and automobile. During the ceremony, I could hear my grandchildren in the crowd. I was so proud and happy, and I smiled so much that my face hurt. I didn't go to the graduation. The hooding and my diploma were enough. I had reached my first goal. As a graduation gift, my daughter Jo had written a poem for me that summed up my life up until this time.

"Ghost Girl"

Little girl on a fence,
Alone, she watched and yearned
for someone to love.
She cried alone at night.
No one heard.
She reached for dreams that
dissolved when she awoke.
She died along with her girlish ideals.
Out of the ashes of her funeral pyre
rose a woman of strength and resolve,
determined that no more innocent dreams
would die.

The woman follows her chosen path
through conflict and pain.
I mourn the little girl who died,
and rejoice for the woman
she has become.
—*Jo Overton*

Fourteen

SEARCHING FOR MY FUTURE

Shortly before graduation, I had put in applications to work with several Legal Services offices. I received a letter telling me that DNA Legal Services, located in Window Rock, Arizona, had scheduled several interviews for me. I was really excited because I'd never been to Navajo country, and it was my first opportunity to explore practicing law in Indian country.

I had to plan my trip carefully because I had several interviews in different places on the Navajo Reservation: Farmington, Chinle, Mexican Hat, and Window Rock. There would be miles and miles of nothing in between them and I'd be driving alone.

On the appropriate day, I got up early and headed west on Interstate 40. I turned off the interstate at Thoreau and drove to Farmington, New Mexico. The city is located in the beautiful San Juan Valley and in easy driving distance to Aztec ruins and other attractions of the Four Corners. At any other time in my life I would have been pleased to have lived there, but I wasn't there to go sightseeing. It was obvious that the people I would be serving would not necessarily be Indians. Was my goal to just serve Indian people, or was I the kind of person who could fulfill Legal Services's goal to end poverty for all people?

I finished the interview and drove on toward Mexican Hat. Monument Valley was as beautiful and impressive as I'd heard it was. As I approached the village, the rugged rock formations were reminiscent of ancient temple spires reaching for the skies and reminding me of the smallness of human beings. As I drove down the road, heat waves shimmered in front of me and a hawk soared high above. I was overwhelmed with the beauty, but I didn't have a camera and I had very little time to stop and admire it all. I stopped long enough to conclude my interview at the small Legal Services office and left wondering how I would handle the isolation and the heat.

I drove on to Chinle, which struck me as being more comparable to Rosebud than the other places I had visited. It was larger than Rosebud, but it had more Indian people than the other towns. The attorneys in Chinle were very welcoming. They showed me around town and assured me that, while housing was at a premium, they would make sure I would have a place to live. I spent the night at the home of one of them and after another visit to the office, they gave me directions to Canyon de Chelly. I didn't have time to go down into the canyon, but as I stood on the rim, awe overcame me. I looked at the ruins built into the walls of the canyon and thought about the ancient people who had lived there and the people who had followed them. I could soon be serving them. I felt humbled by the very idea. I knew I was in a position to make a difference to people who really needed me and at the same time, I thought, "Who am I to be able to do this?"

As I wound my way to my final interview in Window Rock, Arizona, I went back over the last two days, thinking about the places I'd seen and the people I'd met. Everyone had spoken about the service they provided and the goals of Legal Services to provide equal justice and thereby, to end poverty. It appealed to my idealism. I knew I'd be happy working for DNA Legal Services.

At the Window Rock office, which I assumed was the main office, I was interviewed again, but with a difference. This time, they made certain that I knew the downsides of working in Navajo country. It wasn't anything I wasn't familiar with except the cultural differences. I left, feeling encouraged and happy.

Back in Albuquerque, I received a letter from Nevada Indian Legal Services asking me to call them to set up a telephone interview. I had called South Dakota and found that they had no openings. Nevada was very appealing.

After graduation, I had to study for the New Mexico bar exam and pass it to be able to work at all and I started studying for it immediately. It was around-the-clock studying again. We went to classes reviewing the last three years of material and aimed specifically at the subjects that would be covered in the exam. We studied the intricacies of passing the exam and then we took practice exams. It was overwhelming and nerve wracking.

During the second week of Bar Review I got a letter from Nevada Indian Legal Services with a job offer. Not having heard from DNA Legal Services, I called Nevada and accepted the job. Now I had real motivation to pass the bar exam.

Shortly after I accepted the job, one of my classmates came up to me and said, "If you want the job at DNA, you'd better call them."

I was surprised. Evidently, we had a miscommunication. I didn't remember anyone at DNA making a job offer. It boosted my ego to know I had a choice, but I felt obligated to Nevada Indian Legal Services.

Terese was barely a year into her recovery from the car accident. True to my belief that I had to be sure she was independent, I had made her responsible for her daughter's care even though she was in a wheelchair. I insisted that she find an apartment of her own. It wasn't easy for either of us. She was positive she couldn't take care of herself or her baby. I felt so badly for her, but I couldn't let her know how worried I was. I just kept telling her I knew she could do it as we looked for an apartment for her. Her future was at stake. Anita had just graduated from high school and was working and going to classes at UNM. She had her own apartment and, although I worried about her living on her own, I was proud of her. Jan was married and had a baby. I had warned the girls that they would have to be independent by the time I graduated, and they all did it.

I have been asked how I raised such strong, independent daughters and my answer is, "by believing in them."

I took the bar exam at the end of July and immediately began packing for Nevada. I was excited and sad at the same time. I would be on my own, without my girls. I packed my U-Haul truck once again, with the girls' help. I wanted to leave my car for the girls so, once more, I would have to buy a car at my destination. As I drove down Interstate 40, I cried. I thought about all we had been through over the years and I prayed that my girls would be okay on their own. I felt guilty for leaving them and proud that they were all independent. Anita would eventually move back to Sacramento while Jan and Terese would stay in Albuquerque for a time. All four girls would go to college and get degrees.

I drove the truck slowly across Hoover Dam, trying to take in the awe-inspiring sight of the dam while negotiating the narrow roadway. It was frightening, and I was so relieved when I came off the dam and drove to the top of a small hill. As I started down the hill, I stepped on the brake to slow my progress because I could see a traffic light at the bottom of the hill. A busy highway crossed in front of me and I could see heavy traffic headed into Las Vegas.

The brake pedal went all the way to the floor and the truck did not slow down. Frantically, I pumped the brake pedal but nothing happened. The truck just kept rolling. I could see the busy intersection in the distance. My heart was racing as I began to look around in panic. As I got closer to the bottom of the hill, I noticed that there was a mound of gravel on the right side. Without really thinking about it, I turned the steering wheel and aimed the truck for the middle of the gravel. I didn't know what was going to happen, but it appeared to be a better alternative than running into the intersection where cars were speeding by. Fortunately, the shoulder of the road was fairly smooth and there was no ditch to speak of. As the truck plowed into the gravel, it went slower and slower until it finally came to a stop. I was so relieved I put my head down on the steering wheel and cried. When I stopped shaking, I walked across the highway to a convenience store to use the telephone. It wasn't long before a man from the U-Haul company in Las Vegas came to rescue me. I spent the rest of the day waiting for them to evaluate and repair the brakes on the truck.

The next day, I started over again. It took about eight hours to drive to Carson City, where I would live for the next two years. I stayed in a motel for a couple of days while I looked for an apartment and a car. It was fairly easy because Carson City is a small town compared to Albuquerque.

Nevada Indian Legal Services was based on the third floor of an office building. There were two attorneys and I would serve as the third. Within two months of arriving, I got notice that I had passed the New Mexico bar exam. I was officially a lawyer! I called Teewee in Sacramento and the entire family drove up to help me celebrate. The state of Nevada would allow me to practice law under my New Mexico license for two years, after which I would have to take the Nevada bar exam.

Shortly after that, I got notice that I had been selected for the Reginald Heber Smith Community Lawyer Fellowship Program, which was awarded to Legal Services attorneys who qualified. It meant that my salary would be paid for a year and I got a trip to Washington, DC, for training.

Washington was amazing. We had time to go sightseeing, and I couldn't get enough of the history. We ate and shopped in Georgetown, a place I never dreamed I'd ever see. Of course we went to see the monuments, and I went alone to see some portions of the Smithsonian. The Metro scared me, and I was proud of myself for being so daring as to ride it and actually get where I wanted to go.

One of my classmates from UNM was there and since we were all newly minted lawyers, it was a continuing celebration of our achievement. We were immersed in the Legal Services culture and by the time we left, we had a pretty good idea what "poverty law" meant. We were all very enthusiastic about what we'd be doing and we went back to our respective homes with renewed devotion.

Nevada Indian Legal Services was established to serve the Indian tribes scattered through rural Nevada. We also served indigent people throughout Nevada, but we made special efforts to provide service to tribes and their people. Sometimes we traveled to nearby tribal courts to defend people in criminal and civil cases, but much of our work was in educating the people about the legal systems they had to deal with: federal, state, and tribal. It was rewarding and exactly what I wanted. People with knowledge are armed to fight their everyday battles.

The managing attorney was named Sharon and we became very good friends. Dick, the other associate attorney, was tall, witty, and an expert in federal Indian law. Since I was fresh out of law school and knew little or nothing about practicing law, I was in training. Once we became friends, Sharon and Dick told me that they felt fortunate to have me working with them because I could provide a connection to the Indian community. It was a give-and-take relationship, and it was a huge benefit to me. Dick was kind and gentle with a bit of sarcasm thrown in. He would make me laugh when I made mistakes, for which I was very grateful. He shared his extensive knowledge of Indian law, and I gave him advice about connecting with Indian people. Sharon, as the managing attorney, had the main responsibility of showing me the ropes. At first I just tagged along behind her to watch and learn, but I was soon taking my own cases. I learned to write pleadings, interview clients, and how to behave in court.

After a time, they both began to make sure that I was involved in more complex litigation. From them, I learned the real meaning of research and writing. I participated in a Federal Circuit Court case to decide whether the Indian Health Service (IHS) was a primary or secondary payer. It was an important case, and I was proud to have my name included as one of the attorneys.

Most of our cases were garden-variety family law cases—divorce and custody cases that weren't complicated, but often proved to be time-consuming and a lot of work. I learned how to handle emotional clients and how to tell someone they can't have what they want. I learned that you can't get emotionally involved if you hope to give your best to clients. Someone has to be rational!

I developed relationships with people in the Indian communities as we went into the tribal courts. It was a little confusing sometimes because they seldom had professional people in court and the rules got skewed. We did our best to advise them and help improve the situation.

Sharon and I spent a lot of time together as we drove into the far reaches of Nevada to provide service to some very isolated tribes. I had never had contact with Piute or Shoshone people, so I was pleased to get to know some of them. Once, we drove to the Duck Water Shoshone Reservation and spent the day there. They welcomed us with a meal and traditional hand games. They were very isolated and took care of their internal conflicts themselves. We let them know we were always available if they needed help and gave legal advice to several individuals. Before we left them, they showed us an archeological dig nearby. It was a dig in progress, unearthing the remains of giant fish fossils embedded in a hillside of the Nevada desert.

Sharon and I developed a friendship after work, and I settled in to life in Carson City. I would occasionally drive to Sacramento to spend the weekend with Teewee. Sometimes Johnny would show up and we'd have a family dinner. I would have been happy to stay in Nevada, but after nearly two years I discovered that Dakota Plains Legal Services had an opening in South Dakota. Home was calling me.

Fifteen

RETURN TO THE CULTURE

I flew home in June 1987. Getting off the plane in Rapid City, I reached the bottom of the steps and looked out over the green rolling hills of the prairie. I knew that somewhere in the distance the Black Hills rose out of that prairie. Dark with the evergreen trees that covered them, Lakota people had named them *He Sápa*. I looked at them with new eyes, remembering that many people had died for them. Revered by my ancestors, they are still sacred ground to Sioux people. After my long history of city life, the open space gave me a sense of peace and made me think of my childhood. I was home at last.

As I settled into my job at Dakota Plains Legal Services (DPLS), I realized how few connections I had to the community. Three of my brothers were gone, and I didn't know their children very well. I set about trying to renew my family connections. Gratefully, I turned to Jim's family for company. His wife, Lydia, was a teacher and she would become my teacher as well.

As I visited with the family, I came to know that Lydia had been raised by her grandparents who were very traditional. She spoke fluent Lakota and had attended Catholic school so we had similar backgrounds. She had a rich store of knowledge about Lakota culture and the language, which she was happy to share.

During this period of time, I developed a friendship with a woman named Tillie Black Bear, who would have a tremendous impact on my life. It all began when she asked me to help draft a new domestic abuse law. She was the executive director of the White Buffalo Calf Woman Society. The society wanted a new law that would require a mandatory arrest when there was reason for police to believe an assault had taken place. It was necessary because the police would often "counsel" the couple and then leave the victim, usually a woman, to cope with what could be a dangerous situation. We did draft the law and eventually it was passed by the tribal council.

In the meantime, I learned more about Lakota spirituality and domestic violence from Tillie. She felt strongly that a return to traditional ways was necessary to eradicate the violence that had developed on the reservation. The first thing she did for me was to invite me to *Inipi*.[1] I was nervous because I didn't know what to expect, and I felt guilty that I was so ignorant. As I crawled into the sweat lodge, I was in awe. I felt so grateful to be there, which is exactly the right mental state for the ceremony. I thought about Mom and how she had missed it and about Dad, whom I knew had taken part in these ceremonies. As we sat in the circle, the fire tender gently brought in the rocks that would help create the steam. Great care is taken in the selection of the stones to be sure they won't crack or shatter. As the rocks were put in place, our sweat leader, Nadine Thunder Hawk, sprinkled them with prayers and medicinal herbs that crackled and sparked, sending their aroma into the air. With the door closed, Nadine sang the old songs and we each prayed out loud as water was gently poured on the hot rocks, sending up clouds of steam. As I listened to the other women's prayers, I was enveloped in feelings of peace and absolute calm, feelings I'd never felt in any church. The prayers were always heartfelt. Sometimes they were prayers of gratitude and sometimes they were heartrending requests for relief from pain. Sometimes the person who was praying would cry and we'd all cry with her.

Prayers finished, the door was opened for a short time and we talked to each other in low tones until the door closed again. This was repeated four times, and I reminded myself that this was the same way it had always been. I felt connected to the people around me and to my ancestors who had given us this ceremony.

I participated in *Inipi* many times, and my favorites by far were those conducted in the dead of winter. With snow on the ground, sometimes by the light of the moon, we would gather around the fire until we were ready to go into the lodge. We'd shiver our way inside and wait anxiously while the rocks were brought in. Once the door was closed, we were warmed in body and soul. It was wonderful and I will remember it forever.

I became more involved in the White Buffalo Calf Woman Society when I became a member of the board of directors. The society was formed in 1972 when a group of women became concerned about the women on the reservation who didn't have a safe place to go when they were threatened with domestic violence. It would become the very first shelter for women in Indian country. With my board membership came education.

First, I learned about the White Buffalo Calf Woman. Her story has been told many times, in different ways. It is central to the spiritual beliefs of the Lakota people. The story goes that two Lakota warriors were out hunting on the prairie when they saw a beautiful woman, dressed in white buckskin, standing alone. One of the men had feelings of desire for her and when he approached her, they were enveloped in a white cloud of dust or smoke. When it cleared, he was dead and the woman explained that she had been sent as a teacher. She told the second man to go back to camp and to have the chiefs perform certain preparations for when she would arrive there. He complied and the preparations were completed. When the woman appeared in the camp, she set about teaching the people seven rituals to honor *Tunkašila*.[2] One of the rituals was the *Canupa*, the sacred pipe, and she taught them how to use it. When she was finished, as she walked away from the camp, she turned into a white buffalo calf and ran away.

The White Buffalo Calf Woman Society's mission was and is to end violence on the reservation(s). To that end, the society offered the first shelter for battered women in Indian country. All women, regardless of race or creed, were welcome and they came from every direction. They were housed, fed, and clothed until they could decide on the next step in their lives. It was a place of safety and respite.

At first, all I did was to volunteer at the shelter. Having close contact with the women, I looked into the face of fear and I could see myself in years past. I knew every woman's belief that she was so worthless and stupid that she could not take care of herself or her children on her own. I understood that she wanted to believe he still loved her and that things could change because it was all her fault anyway. She would do better and he wouldn't hit her again. Yes, she would probably go back to him and try again.

Sitting on the board of directors, I absorbed the philosophy of the society: offer as much help as possible, but do not interfere or criticize. When a woman decides to leave her batterer, she may be in danger because he will likely be enraged. Only she knows the depth of that danger and whether the time is right for her. Counseling doesn't include trying to advise her on how to fix her relationship. She is only given information about how best to keep herself safe and how to leave safely. If she decides to leave him for good, she will be given help and emotional support to start a new life.

Relationships, like mine, don't necessarily start out in a victim-aggressor situation. It can develop over time with the normal give and take of a couple. If each person is not totally aware and caring about the needs of the other, one person can over run and dominate the other, leaving them unhappy but unable to voice it.

When my husband hit me the first time, I was shocked and traumatized and I began to act like a victim. I was afraid of him, and I showed it. I believe that when I lost my ability to stand up to him, he realized that I was vulnerable and his behavior became increasingly aggressive. Soon, he didn't have to hit me. All he had to do was threaten.

I also learned that violence is likely to escalate once it starts. There are definite signs when disagreements begin to deteriorate into abuse. It usually starts with "small" things: name-calling and criticism, which will escalate into pushing and grabbing and then to real hitting. It will all increase in intensity over time. Most of the time the victim will be told it's her fault and she will come to believe it.

Lakota culture was always centered on respect—respect for one's self and for others. Unfortunately, we seem to have drifted away from that. It's my belief that boarding schools are to blame. We were taught violence at the hands of the adults who were supposed to take care of us. An entire generation came out of boarding school believing that violent punishment was the way to teach a child. We were all thrown together without the loving guidance of our parents to teach us how to get along with each other. We started off thinking we had to hit to defend our persons and our possessions, and we learned to include name-calling and foul language to hurt the other person.

Violence against women in particular began with the coming of the white man. In Lakota society, although there were few women warriors, women were respected for the necessary part they played in the survival of the tribe. Women owned the *t'ípis* and their contents, and they helped decide when to move. I believe that attitudes began to change when

Indian men saw that white women were not treated equally and were, in fact, prohibited from making decisions. The idea of women's inequality was solidified when the treaty makers demanded that only men be allowed to sign. Boarding school taught us all how to take advantage of anyone who was weak, and we've passed it on, generation to generation.

One summer, after a sweat, Tillie asked me if I would consider "going up on the hill," the colloquial term for the *hanbleceya* ceremony.[3] I was taken aback, overwhelmed with a feeling of humility. How could she think I was worthy to participate in it? I couldn't speak Lakota, and I felt I didn't know enough about the culture or the spiritual practices. I was, after all, still learning. I was so honored that she would teach me and help me through this ceremony.

The instruction started with me making a star quilt to take with me. Star quilts are made in the pattern to represent the Morning Star and are traditionally used in ceremonies. I can't remember how long it took to make the quilt, but I do remember that Lydia and I went to a class to learn a short-cut method to make star quilts. I filled my quilt with heavy batting, knowing that our *hanbleceya* would take place in June when the nights are still pretty cold.

During the time I was making my quilt, I learned to make tobacco prayer ties. I cut small squares of red material and put tobacco in the middle. I rolled it up and tied it around the middle with string. The string would be used to attach the next tie and then the next, until there was a string of ties. As I made each tie, I said a prayer. Usually, the medicine man would tell us how many ties were necessary for a particular ceremony. The strings of ties would be used to encircle the area where the ceremony took place.

Participants in *hanbleceya* become carriers of the sacred pipe. It's not to be taken lightly because there is much responsibility in owning a pipe. I got instructions on the meaning of the pipe, how to use it, and how to take care of it. I was impressed and awed.

During the time I was waiting for my *hanbleceya*, I had to pay close attention to what I was doing and thinking. The requirement is to have positive behavior, good thoughts, and to remember to pray. Alcohol is specifically prohibited.

Later on, we would go to Green Grass, the place where the original pipe is kept by the hereditary Keeper of the Pipe. There were hundreds of pipe carriers who attended a once-in-a- lifetime opportunity to view the original pipe. The pipe was kept wrapped and sheltered in this special place to ensure its security and to prevent its disintegration. Each pipe carrier was given a moment to view, not touch, the pipe. Sacred songs were sung as we all stood in line, waiting our turn. People spoke in hushed tones, and the atmosphere was one of reverence and controlled excitement.

Normally, a *hanbleceya* takes at least four days and nights. The participant is alone, and no food or water is allowed. Tillie and I had decided we would go up at the same time but in separate places. Since we were both unwell and required medication for our illnesses, it was decided we would limit ourselves to twenty-four hours. I was very nervous about going without my medication, which I took four times a day. I wasn't sure I could do it.

We met in the early morning to begin our ceremony. We were taken several miles out to an isolated area. We looked around until we found a clearing in the trees. Green grass and shrubbery made me think about snakes. I put my star quilt on the ground, partially in shade in consideration of the coming heat of the day. The quilt was bordered with small stakes that were strung with the tobacco ties I had made. This enclosure would be my home for the next twenty-four hours. I looked around and Tillie was nowhere in sight. I was alone with my quilt and my pipe.

I sat down with the pipe next to me and examined my surroundings. The trees were mostly evergreen and were not too tall, probably because of a lack of water and good earth. Grass and weeds combined to create a small green meadow where I sat. Small stands of shrubs grew under the trees and were still bare of leaves at this time of year. It was very quiet and the wind was still.

I decided that I needed to clear my mind so I could concentrate on my prayers. I closed my eyes and concentrated on my breathing. The time, place, and circumstance were perfect for meditation. Soon, I was conscious of the reason I was there. I began to pray to Tunkašila to make me worthy of this ceremony and to bring me a vision. I prayed for myself and for the people. Those prayers would be repeated many times in the next twenty-four hours.

As I sat on my quilt, I began to notice that the ground beneath me was very hard. My back was tired from sitting upright and I began to sweat a little. I would lie down for a time to ease my aching back, and I would soon be sitting up again. There were various and sundry bugs flying around, but no flies or bees, thank goodness. As the day wore on, the heat became more intense. I was wearing a Sundance dress, which was made of blue cotton and very loosely fit, but I became very uncomfortable and sweaty. Sometimes I would pull my arms inside the dress to protect them from the sun and still, it was hot, hot, hot. All the discomfort was very distracting. I had difficulty in concentrating on my prayers. I began to worry about the fact that I hadn't been able to take my medication, even though my pain hadn't increased significantly. When I became too distracted or worried, I would switch back to just doing meditation for a short time. I wasn't too hungry, but I was very thirsty and it began to feel as though the day would never end.

I was relieved as the sun began to go down. I could look forward to cooler air. As time went on, I began to ask myself why I had decided to do this. Then I would remind myself that it was something I really wanted to do and that I couldn't give up anyway. There was no one around to rescue me. I thought about calling out to see if Tillie was close enough to hear me, but I never did it.

I would just redouble my efforts to keep praying and tell myself, "I can do this."

As night fell, there was a chill in the air. At first it was comfortable, and the evening went fine. Then it began to get dark and cold, and my physical discomfort increased. There was no moon, and the only light was starlight. I marveled at the dark beauty of the sky as I lay on my back looking through the trees. My joints began to ache, and I had renewed fear that it was going to become unbearable. I tried curling into a fetal position to warm myself, but there was little relief. I would start to pray and I'd nod off to sleep, whether I was sitting or lying down. I wrapped the quilt around myself, glad I'd been generous with the batting. It was still cold and real, deep sleep never came. In the dark of the night, I was never afraid. I prayed and thought about how lucky I was to be there.

With the dawn came the realization that it would soon be over. I thought about the hours that had passed and asked myself whether I had done what I set out to do. I decided that I hadn't been conscientious enough about my prayers and that twenty-four hours were not enough to constitute a true vision quest, but I was so grateful to have had the experience.

By the time they came to get me, the sun was climbing in the sky and it was getting warm. We went directly to *Inipi* to give thanks and I shared my pipe for the first time. I gave my quilt to one of the women who had helped with the preparations and the sweat. We all shared a meal of soup and fry bread, and I drove home, grateful and feeling very connected to my parents and grandparents. As I drove down the road, I thought that this was a road that Mom and Dad had driven down and these were the trees and meadows they had seen. These were the people they knew and I could know them, too.

Sixteen

LIVING THE DREAM

The Dakota Plains Legal Services (DPLS) office was located in Mission, on the reservation. Growing up, I had actually spent very little time there. White River was not part of the reservation. In the beginning, the town was an Episcopal mission. Located just twelve miles from the Rosebud Agency, it has remained the largest community on the reservation. There are nineteen other communities that make up the Rosebud Reservation.

There were four other attorneys in the office to serve several thousand people. During the time I was there, the majority of our clients were tribal members, but we also took care of anyone who was poor and needed legal assistance. Some of them were local farmers and ranchers.

I was rather disappointed when I discovered that this office wasn't nearly as friendly or helpful as Nevada Indian Legal Services had been. The support staff were all Indians and were experienced and helpful. I learned more from them than any of the attorneys. I spent a lot of time in the law library, looking for information I could have gotten from an experienced attorney. Working conditions were not pleasant and I missed my mentors in Nevada.

In spite of the difficulties of working at DPLS, I set about reconnecting to my community. In those days, Legal Services was geared toward organizing people, when necessary, to try to change social problems and make their lives better. Housing was and is a tremendous problem on reservations. Bernie, a paralegal, and I worked on a landlord-tenant organization, trying to empower the people to demand better housing conditions. We did our best to change the law which, at that time, favored the rights of landlords. As much as I had loved my job in Carson City, I was passionate about the people of Rosebud. I knew I'd be around for a long time, perhaps to see the fruits of my labor.

After two years of working at DPLS, I quit my job because it was so obvious that they disliked me and would never allow me to grow in the organization. In addition, Legal Services was changing. The funding was cut and we were restricted in the kinds of cases we could handle. We couldn't represent groups of people any more. My chance to learn how to handle more complicated cases disappeared. When my application for a position as managing attorney for one of the other offices was denied, I decided to leave.

I left DPLS in 1989 and accepted a position as prosecutor for the Rosebud Sioux Tribe. I enjoyed the work because it gave me a chance to learn criminal law. For the most part, my cases were simple: driving under the influence, simple assault, and such. During the last couple of months of my tenure, I had to investigate the case of a tribal member who was accused of molesting his own children. At the time, such things were deep, dark secrets that no one ever talked about. I didn't get to finish the case because I changed jobs and the man was never prosecuted. My heart still aches for those children who have never admitted that anything happened. A shameful secret is a wound that never heals.

Looking back, I can see that I was always looking for new challenges. I had to keep learning new things. Nothing made me happier than getting a new case with issues about which I knew nothing. I grew to love the law library at the state capitol. I was always there after hours when no one else was around except maybe a lone lawyer with his head buried in a book. It was quiet and a bit spooky sometimes. As I left the capitol building, my footsteps would echo in the empty hallways. I always felt a sense of wonder that I was there—and best of all, I belonged there!

At the end of 1989, I was appointed the first Attorney General of the Rosebud Sioux Tribe. When I was interviewed by the tribal council, one of the councilmen (in those days there were few women on the council) asked me whether I was sure I wouldn't cry in court if it was difficult. He was clearly contemptuous of women, and I began to realize that misogyny and chauvinism were part of reservation life.

Alex Lunderman Sr. was president, and he loved going to Washington, DC, to lobby Congress. He had a great support staff who kept him informed and helped him navigate the rough waters of federal politics. I accompanied him on several occasions and our party moved swiftly, keeping prearranged appointments to address the numerous issues of tribal government. It made me realize how important it is for a president to have a skilled support staff. Gerri Arcoren was the best. Alex was a recovering alcoholic and although he dressed in baggy khakis and plaid shirts, he was always sober, serious, and dedicated to his job. I was happy to be one of his advisors.

I had my own secretary, Marie, who was efficient and organized. Our office was made up of two tiny rooms, but we did have windows. I was so proud of the tribe for being progressive, and I felt that my most important job would be to help ensure that the civil rights of the people would be upheld. I felt that I was carrying Bob's legacy to fruition.

One day I asked a coworker if she knew where I could get some bricks. I was living in a rented mobile home that had a decorative brick wall that needed repair.

She said, "There is a pile of bricks out where the old boarding school used to be."

The day I drove out to the old campus, it was hot and windy. A little whirlwind of dust skipped its way across the dirt road on the campus. I looked up at the old water tower and remembered when Johnny and his buddies climbed to the top when they were supposed to be training for a track meet. There were remnants of the old boiler/laundry room that brought back memories of kids staggering under huge bundles of dirty sheets. The only building left intact was the dining hall.

The pile of bricks was obvious. They sat there, in a pile, some whole and some broken into little pieces. They were situated on the northwest corner of the old quad, the old location of the girls' building. I stooped to pick up a brick and I could see the old building in my mind. I saw the small green lawn and the iron pipes that formed a railing around it. I remembered sitting on the railing, waiting for a chance to see my brother. Tears filled my eyes and I couldn't hold onto the brick. I dropped it, got back into my car, and drove away.

A short time after my appointment as Attorney General, the tribal council passed an ordinance requiring all businesses on the reservation to buy a business license. It wasn't a surprise because the council was required to publish notice before the law could go into effect. We knew there would be some controversy and that the non-Indian business owners would resist.

The tribal council decided that they would call a meeting for all the business owners, including the non-Indians, to inform them about the new law. The meeting was advertised, and we prepared for a confrontation. When we walked into the room, the hostility was palpable. The chairs were filled and men stood leaning against the walls. We were outnumbered, but we knew we had the law on our side. We wanted to let them know that while we had the upper hand, we had no intention of misusing our power. We just wanted to educate them about the requirements of the law and what we would be doing to enforce it. It was my job, as Attorney General, to answer questions. I was nervous because council members were ready for confrontation and the non-Indians were on the defensive. This could be nasty.

As it turned out, there were some strident exchanges, but their questions were answered and we left, knowing they would comply with the new law. Well, most of them would comply. There were a few who tried to hold out, insisting that they would not be ruled by Indians. I filed suit, in the name of the tribe, to force them to buy business licenses, and eventually everyone accepted the fact that Rosebud did indeed have jurisdiction over them. It was a new day, and we were jubilant!

Prior to my becoming Attorney General, the tribe filed a lawsuit in Federal Court to stop the State of South Dakota from asserting jurisdiction over the highways on the reservation. The Federal District Court ruled that South Dakota had jurisdiction and the tribe appealed to the Eighth Circuit Court of Appeals. While the appeal was pending, the president and tribal council daringly issued what amounted to an executive order stating that the state highway patrol would be barred from coming onto the reservation. The State filed a motion to hold the tribe in contempt. They contended that the order was a violation of the District Court's decision.

One day, at a council meeting, there was a discussion about what would happen if the Court found the tribe in contempt. I explained to them that the usual punishment for contempt was a fine, imprisonment, or both. They absolutely loved that! They became very excited and began to talk about going to jail. The discussion became very boisterous as they envisioned themselves in jail. Someone brought up the possibility that we could put up toll gates at each of our borders.

One of the councilmen asked whether or not I was going to jail with them. I told them that it wasn't a possibility. As a lawyer, licensed by the State of South Dakota, I could not violate my oath by disobeying a court order. I explained that my license to practice might be put in jeopardy by such an act and that I was unwilling to risk it. It was a serious matter to me. I didn't realize it right away, but my refusal to participate in an imagined jail sentence was seen as disloyalty by some council members.

The entire matter ended when the Court issued an order dismissing the State's motion for contempt. Eventually, the council met with the state highway patrol and informed them that the tribe did not need them to control our highways. The highway patrol agreed based on the fact that their budget would benefit. Many years later, the councilman who had asked the question once again brought the matter up on the council floor. I believe his purpose was to try to embarrass me. I was astounded that after twenty-plus years, it was still an issue. I stood up and restated my reasons for refusing to go along with the jail idea, although it was clear that the current council wasn't the least bit interested in the old story. Later that day, I approached the gentleman, shook his hand and told him I thought that holding a grudge for twenty years was unhealthy.

I tell this rather complicated story because it says a lot about tribal politics. My refusal to consider going to jail was my undoing and the end of my dream of enforcing civil rights on the reservation.

With a new election, we got a new president and some new council members. When the air cleared, I discovered that they had zeroed out the budget for the Attorney General's office. I was without a job. The new president very contemptuously said to me, "Go down there and be a judge. That's where you belong." He was telling me to go to the courthouse and become a judge. This comment was indicative of the attitude of tribal politicians toward our judicial system. I wasn't good enough to be the Attorney General, but I could be a judge.

In those days, many tribal judges didn't have a degree of any kind. Without the law to guide them, judges made decisions based on personal opinion and woe to those who opposed a judge's friend or relative. My own father was a tribal judge before I was born, appointed by the

Bureau of Indian Affairs (BIA). I suppose he, too, allowed himself to be influenced. It was part of the job.

I wasn't going to let anyone tell me what to do, so I decided to start my own practice. For the next four years, I struggled to make a living. I became a court-appointed attorney in criminal cases in state court and represented people in divorce, custody, probate, and other civil cases. The biggest difficulty was in getting people to pay me what they owed. I looked for work with other tribes. I became tribal judge for the Yankton Sioux Tribe and at various times I was their prosecutor or public defender.

These positions were let out for bid by the BIA, and at one point I filed a complaint because the Indian man who supposedly out bid me was close friends with the agency superintendent and was given $300 more than me. He had graduated from law school but was not licensed to practice law in any state. He was also very rude to me in court, and it was obvious that he was giving preferential treatment to the white attorney who worked with me. It seemed that no matter where I went, on any reservation, being a woman was detrimental.

During this time, people were complaining about the new president for Rosebud. Some of us got together and decided that we would oust him. In order to do that, we needed to file a petition to recall him. We put our heads together and decided on a list of reasons for recall. My own reason was that he was unfamiliar with our constitution and had no respect for it.

It's not uncommon on the reservation for people to be unhappy with a new regime. It is uncommon for anyone to try to remove a president. What followed was an education in organization and tribal politics.

Once we gathered a core group of about six people, we had to educate everyone on the requirements of the petition. We had to map out where we would go and when. Since the towns and communities on the reservation are very widespread, we had to make sure everyone had money for gas. Most of us had jobs so our signature gathering was done in the evenings and on weekends. In the short time that we had to gather signatures, some of us became good friends. We were serious about what we were doing, but we had fun doing it. In the process we learned about our tribal constitution and its flaws. We passed those lessons on to the people we met and encouraged them to pay attention to tribal politics and to vote.

In the end, we were able to gather the required amount of signatures and there was a hearing of sorts before the tribal council. We knew from the start that the petition would be turned over to the tribal council to make a decision as to whether or not our grounds for recall were adequate. We also knew that history was against us. Since the decision was in the hands of the tribal council, it was highly unlikely that they would vote against one of their own. And, that's exactly the way it ended. The experience left me with a determination that one day I would change the law to ensure that the people have more voice in their government.

By 1994, I was dissatisfied with my life. I didn't feel like I was helping anyone, and I was tired of being economically strapped. I started looking for another job. I applied and was granted an interview at the University of New Mexico, School of Law. The position was to be the director of the Indian Law Clinical Program. I was so excited about going to Albuquerque again, but I was more excited to be part of their Indian Law program.

It was great to walk into the law school again, feeling that I really belonged there. It was good to talk to some of my old professors knowing I was on equal footing with them (well, almost.) The interview went well, but in the end I was told that I was their second choice. Their first choice was a Zuni woman who came from the area and was a natural choice. Still, I was pleased that my alma mater had considered me for the job. Shortly after that, I got a second chance. I put in an application for a position at the University of California, Oak River Law School.

When the announcement came that I had been chosen for an interview, I was excited. It was a prestigious law school in California, and I felt honored once again. They would consider me for an administrative position in their Law Clinic for Native Americans. My self-esteem soared. I knew this was a job that I was fully capable of carrying off. It was a little scary because it would be a job I had not done before, but I was sure enough of my ability to adapt and I knew I had the people skills required to manage a program. I was excited by the prospect of adding to my repertoire of professional skills.

I had applied for the position because the advertisement in the newspaper listed qualifications that I had. The Law Clinic for Native Americans wanted someone who had a background in Indian Law and who'd had experience working with Legal Services or poverty law programs. It was me, to a "T." I had practiced Indian Law in Indian country for nearly ten years and part of those years was spent working with Indian people, representing them in poverty law issues.

I flew to Los Angeles, California, on a sunny day. As the shuttle took me to Oak River, I was inundated by civilization. There were so many buildings and highways that I missed the beauty of the ocean and the mountains all around me.

At my hotel, I discovered that my room was a suite. I'd never slept in a suite before, and I was really impressed. I felt like a real "rez" kid, mouth open and gawking.

Early the next morning, I was scheduled to have breakfast with the university search team who would interview me. I felt honored and humbled when I realized they had done a national search for job candidates. I was introduced to Georgiana Browning, the chairwoman of the board of directors for the Law Clinic for Native Americans, and Thomas Rawley, professor of Indian Law and author of an Indian Law textbook. There were others, but sadly I don't remember them specifically after all these years.

The interview was casual as I answered their questions about what I had done and asked my own questions about the job. I was told that, although the clinic had a director, he had agreed that he would leave in favor of a Native American director. I was left with the impression that this was a prestigious job and would fulfill all my expectations. I would be able to teach and to influence future lawyers to help Indian people and their tribes.

The interview ended with them asking if I wanted the job. When I said yes, Professor Rawley grabbed my hand and, to my embarrassment, said he couldn't believe I was actually coming to work for them. I felt pretty lucky myself.

Oak River, California, is rather a unique city. I couldn't have chosen a place more far removed from my home environment and my comfort zone. Someone told me that Oak River, "is ten square miles of fantasy surrounded by reality." Nearly everyone who lives there imagines themselves living a life of luxury, whether or not they actually have money. I found an apartment in Ivy Creek, not too far from the university, and started my job.

The university itself is an incubator for all the excesses of American life. Many students come from privileged backgrounds and enroll themselves into an atmosphere of a playland. They seemed to concentrate on skiing, rafting, surfing, hiking, and so on, and drinking and drugs were and are rampant. Our serious law students played, too, but not as assiduously as the undergrads. Native American students complained about the complete lack of diversity, although the university administration bragged about their efforts to change that.

I should have known that this law school was like any other, including UNM. The only problem was that I was now on the other side of the political game and in unfamiliar territory. The Law Clinic for Native Americans was, I believe, fairly new. I wasn't given any information, by either the director or the board, about how the clinic was run. I didn't ask too many questions about the hierarchy of the university because I assumed I'd find out in due time. Instead, I found myself in a quandary with no one to turn to for advice. After it was all over, I found out that the board of directors was just an advisory board. They, evidently, had plans for the clinic, but no control over how those plans would be implemented. The clinic was supposed to be part of the board's plan to expand the university's reputation as a leader in Indian Law. The clinic director was hired by the university's board of regents and answered to the dean of the law school.

The clinic was new and was treated like a red-headed stepchild by the rest of the faculty. I was mystified when I introduced myself to the librarian and she looked at me with disdain, refusing to show me around the library.

However, the course was not considered to be rigorous by university standards, and the clinic staff wasn't considered to be part of the faculty. It didn't bother me because I seldom saw any of the other faculty, and my motivation for being there was different than theirs. Our offices were in the basement, figuratively and literally.

I fell completely in love with the students. Most of them were Indians from across the nation, young and excited about being in law school. There were a few who were white and anxious to help bring justice to Indian country. Most of them were urban Indians who had never lived on a reservation. I couldn't wait to tell them how it was to practice law in Indian country and apply their knowledge of Indian Law to make things better.

One day the director invited me to attend the class he conducted. I enjoyed the class although I was a little nervous about teaching law students. I knew there would be some that would challenge me. The director interrupted me several times, and I felt more like a participant or visitor than a teacher. I didn't think too much about it. I thought he was just giving me time to acclimate myself to the routine and the situation. I was wrong.

After a while it became evident that the director didn't know what I knew—that I was supposed to replace him. He acted as though I was just there to be his assistant. We had our first disagreement over what my title should be. I insisted that it reflect my status as the future director and he didn't agree. He eventually compromised and I was called co-director.

Even my office reflected my status. I was told there was no money to paint the dirty walls or fix the broken window blinds. The office furniture didn't come close to the standards I had come to expect as a lawyer and judge. I was sorely disappointed in every facet of my new position. It all made me wonder what happened and why I was suddenly so unimportant.

I discovered that my duties didn't reflect my expected status either. I never got to teach a class or to supervise the students in working with actual cases. I was assigned to the "prison project," which was ostensibly to help Native American inmates who's right to religious freedom was being denied but was basically a way to placate them. In reality, the prisons do a pretty good job of honoring inmates' right to practice their religion. I didn't appreciate the use of my time. I resented the fact that I was never given the opportunity to review the matters beforehand or to choose which cases I believed were worthy of our attention.

I was also assigned to oversee Indian Child Welfare Act cases.[1] The ICWA was passed by Congress to ensure that Indian children would not be removed from their homes unnecessarily and that those who were removed from their homes would not lose access to their culture. The Law Clinic for Native Americans was looking for important cases that would establish its reputation in Indian Law. The director sent me out to visit a mother who had lost her kids to the state. It turned out that she'd been found guilty of neglect and was having difficulty trying to adhere to the court's orders. She refused to allow her children to be placed in an Indian foster home and there was little I could do beyond providing emotional support. That was our ICWA case, and we never got a call involving a real ICWA violation.

The clinic also wanted a connection to the Southern California Indian community. Who could do it better than a real Indian—me? I remember driving into the far reaches beyond the Los Angeles suburbs to attend a couple of Indian community meetings. They didn't need legal advice and some people resented our intrusion, especially those that had established themselves as leaders in their communities. I knew it was going to take years for the clinic to establish itself as a go-to organization for the Indian community. As a beginning, all we could do was establish our presence to build trust. I was ready to do that, but I would have to learn the politics of the community.

Another of the missions of the clinic was to serve tribes in updating codes and assisting them with other legal problems they might have. The problem was that there are no reservations in close proximity. Considering the clinic's financial standing (practically nonexistent), it was impossible to do outreach in person to get to know tribal leaders and offer our services. I pictured myself introducing myself and the clinic to tribal people who'd never had access to legal assistance and how we could help them. It was never going to happen because the director thought we could just contact them by phone and/or letter, not realizing that it would be necessary to establish mutual respect first.

These were all of the obstacles that I brought to the attention of the director, and I knew it was going to take some long-range planning to accomplish the goals of the clinic, but the director didn't want to hear any of my suggestions. He was focusing his time and attention on teaching the Indian Law class and two or three cases that were already in court. He had no interest in sharing those matters with me. It appeared to me that he resented my being there.

I was deeply disappointed as I discovered that the job wasn't what I thought it would be. My biggest disappointment was that I had so little contact with the students. I wanted to be a teacher. Because most of them were Indian, they gravitated toward me naturally. I was invited into their social circle and became a friend. They would come into my office and talk about their experiences, or lack thereof, with their tribes and families. Some had never had contact with their tribe, and we talked about the protocol for making contact. I remember a young woman who labeled her grandmother a Cherokee Indian Princess, which is a standing joke in Indian country. I felt so badly for her when I found out she was a descendant of John Ross and didn't realize how important he was.[2] She was, indeed, a princess in my eyes.

As time passed, the director's and my relationship became more and more contentious. He thought I was deliberately influencing the students to dislike him. I felt that nothing I was doing was related to practicing law. Almost anyone without a law degree could have done what I was doing. I became resentful and frustrated as I tried to change my status. It became clear to me that the director had no intention of leaving.

The worst part was that I had absolutely no one to turn to. All of my expectations for the job were dashed. I reached out to several people for support, but surprisingly, no one ever encouraged me to stay and wait for their plans to play out. It seemed that the only plan they had was for the director to leave of his own accord.

My last-ditch effort was to talk to the dean; he informed me that the board of regents had already renewed the director's contract. He wasn't going to leave. Why would he? Obviously, these sophisticated people had believed his promise to leave in favor of a Native American and didn't know what to do when he changed his mind. Maybe in time they would have found a way to solve the problem, but in the meantime, I was miserable. I had no idea when his contract expired, and the job was empty and boring. I decided to leave.

I was relieved and happy to go home. I was immediately hired as tribal attorney for the Flandreau Santee Tribe (FSST) at a much better salary than I was getting. Flandreau is a small tribe, and I met many wonderful people there. They had just begun to work on plans for a casino. I worked with the finance officer to secure the financing of the casino, and we traveled to Minneapolis to sign the final papers. I have to admit that it was pretty exciting, dabbling in high finance. It was a lot of money, and I had to be sure everything in the contract was right.

After that, contracts galore crossed my desk. Contracts class in law school was never my favorite, but I was grateful now. We contracted for everything from earth movers to carpets and slot machines, and it brought up issues of Federal Indian Law. I was challenged and happy.

My very favorite role was acting as advisor to Tribal Chairman Richard "Chuck" Allen. He was quiet, sober, and dedicated to his job. When he wasn't quite sure about any issue, we would have a discussion and exchange ideas. We went to Washington, DC, together to lobby Congress.

Chuck walked fast and sometimes I could hardly keep up with him. As we rushed through the long halls of the office buildings, looking for a Congressman's office, I felt humbled and grateful for the opportunity to be of service to the tribe. It was what I had always wanted. Before we went to see any Congressman, we would talk about what we were going to say and what the Congressman might say. Once, we met with Janet Reno, the US Attorney General, to discuss law enforcement issues on the reservation. Tall and stately, she listened respectfully to everyone who was there. When we left, we felt that we had been heard.

Chuck and I also went to a meeting of the National Congress of American Indians. This organization was founded to bring tribes together to communicate with the United States Congress with a unified voice. Once at the meeting, Chuck and I split up, each of us going to meet with different committees in order to have a voice on different issues. After the committees met, there was a plenary session to have all the tribes vote on each issue. I was so pleased to have been able to participate and voice my opinion. At the plenary session, I saw the members of Rosebud's delegation. They came in late and it was obvious that they had been drinking the night before. It wasn't very reassuring about the state of Rosebud's tribal government.

During this time, I began to have more problems with my knees. My orthopedist talked me into having a complete knee replacement. I was so happy with it that I soon replaced the other knee. I could walk without pain for the first time in many, many years. Within months, I was back in the hospital to have an emergency operation on my neck. My top two vertebrae had slipped and my skull was dangerously close to pinching off my spinal cord. After two days of using weights to pull my head back into place, the doctors operated to fuse the two vertebrae. I wore a steel "halo" to hold my head in place for ten weeks. I continued to go to work, and I thank my coworkers for putting up with the way I looked with that contraption on my head.

I stayed at Flandreau for three years and then one of their own tribal members graduated from law school and came home. In a very short time, it became obvious that she was replacing me. Coincidentally, I had a visit from my friend Tillie. She told me that the South Dakota Coalition Against Domestic Violence was looking for an attorney. I was so pleased when I got the job because I would be able to go home to Rosebud.

Seventeen

BACK TO THE PEOPLE

My home became my office, so I bought a house in Mission. My job was to give legal advice to the members of the coalition. The coalition was made up of several shelters for battered women located across the state. I also represented battered women in court for various reasons. It seemed as though it was my destiny to be able to help these women who were victimized and lived in terror.

I went to coalition meetings and met the wonderful women who do this work. They were all like Tillie—passionate and dedicated to their work. Most of them had been abused themselves and fully understood the dilemma of the women they were trying to help.

I visited shelters and gave legal advice to their directors and boards. I talked to the women who lived in the shelters and looked into the face of fear and anguish. I tried to help them understand what their options were. I explained the ramifications of divorce and child custody, and I knew they didn't want the information, but maybe somewhere in the future they would need it and use it.

I met a woman who was running from her abuser along with her children. They had fled from Arizona and she was terrified that he would find her because he was a police officer and had the means to find her. By the time I met her, she had already gone to court somewhere else and had changed her name and those of her children. She wanted to disappear and needed to get a divorce and to change her children's Social Security numbers. None of this is unusual for battered women. It was a difficult process, but my client was determined and resourceful. I couldn't be with her at the divorce hearing and she represented herself, which was just as well since she wanted to do some things that were beyond my ethical boundaries. She was an intelligent woman, and she was granted her divorce and sole custody of her children. She even managed to talk the judge into sealing her divorce proceeding so her husband would never have access to the record. It was her determination and willingness to go it alone that set her free.

I had another client who came into my life after she had gotten a restraining order against her husband. She was trying to decide whether or not to get a divorce. After we talked about it, we decided that I would go ahead and draft the divorce papers. I would wait for her to tell me when, and if, she decided to go through with it. One morning, she called and said that she decided to go forward with the divorce. I reminded her that separation is usually the most dangerous time for a woman in an abusive situation. I asked her to go to the local shelter because I thought he would be enraged when he received the divorce papers. She said that he had not violated the restraining order and she was confident that she would be okay.

The next morning, I got a phone call from the director of the local shelter telling me that my client had been badly beaten that night.

This case launched me into all the complexities of practicing law in Indian country. After all was said and done, the tribal court granted the divorce, the state court settled the custody of their child, and her husband was sentenced to federal prison.

The struggle was protracted and I was impressed by her strength and determination. She never wavered once she made her decision. It required several hearings and much paperwork. I would look at her and I could see fear and pain of loss, and she carried on.

In 2000 I was offered a job on the Pine Ridge Oglala Reservation, working for another growing domestic violence organization. I commuted back and forth and I was on the road on September 11, 2001, when the world changed for all of us. I heard it on the radio, and I looked out over the peaceful prairie, grateful that we were all safe in our own little world.

I enjoyed working with the women, but I became frustrated, and often angry, with the tribal court. It was so dysfunctional that no one could count on the rules or the law. People were allowed to practice in the court without any formal training and it often happened that whoever got to the judge first could get their orders signed. It was also very easy to get an order countermanded. Police officers were ill-trained to do investigations and justice was wanting. We did our best to work around the dysfunction, but I soon got tired of it. And then I had a disagreement with the program administrators and resigned.

I returned to Rosebud to become an associate judge. I was happy to work with Chief Judge Sherman Marshall. Judge Marshall had been chief judge for fifteen years, more or less, and had been instrumental in developing Rosebud's court into a stable system. Early on in his tenure he had confronted the tribal council with his decision to stop political influence in the court. He was called to the council floor when he ordered a mentally ill person committed. The family disagreed and had gone to the council to complain. Before the council, Judge Marshall was ordered to vacate the commitment order and he refused. He told the council he would resign before he would vacate the order. That was the last time the tribal council ever tried to interfere with a court order. Around 2004, the council made it illegal for tribal officials to interfere in court decisions. Separation of powers between the branches of government had begun.

Eighteen

THE WORK GOES ON

I settled into my job as judge. For a time I was the Children's Court judge. My favorite role was that of judge for the Youth Drug Court. We met each week with kids who had committed an offense involving drugs or alcohol. Some were already addicted and others had just begun. They had to pass a drug test and talk about what they had done that week. In the process of talking about their week, I found out about their families and how they were doing in school. Their parents had to attend as well and, for many of them, it was the first time they actually knew how their kids were doing. I don't know what the success rate was, but the process helped everyone. The Drug Court is still active, and I hope that each of the participants comes out knowing that someone cares about them and that they have choices in their lives.

I seldom heard criminal cases, and the civil cases were mostly divorces, child custody, and such. Now and then, there would be a complicated case dealing with jurisdictional or other issues and I enjoyed the challenge. By this time, Rosebud had had a Supreme Court for some time. I was so proud of our court system. In times past, when a new council was sworn in, one or two of them would walk through the court house with an "I can take you down" attitude. That changed with the new law preventing council interference.

The day came when I discovered that one of the court staff was making more money than I was, and it wasn't another judge. He had bypassed the chief judge and bargained with tribal council members. I felt unappreciated and angry. I decided that it would be the last time my tribe would have the opportunity to discount my ability and my worth. I resigned.

Retirement came easy. I joined a women's group that had recently been resurrected. They weren't quite sure what they wanted to do and couldn't decide on a name. As election time approached, our group had an influx of people who were unhappy with tribal government. It soon became obvious that there was a demand for "somebody" to do something about all the problems. We named our group "Lakota Women for Change" and moved forward.

When people found out we were driven by politics, many of them dropped out of the group but continued to use us to voice their concerns. Many tribal members are afraid of the power wielded by the council and don't want to speak up on their own. They fear that the jobs of their friends and family members may be at risk. Also, if some council members don't like you, you may be denied some of the other benefits of being a tribal member.

I don't think we influenced the election, but later we used our collective voices to let the tribal council know that we didn't agree with whatever decision they were about to make. In other words, we were lobbying.

We began to hear from women from other tribes, encouraging us and urging us to continue. As our reputation spread, we began to hear negative comments from some of our male tribal members. I'm sorry to say that those comments were usually aimed at our gender. We laughed and acknowledged that it was to be expected. Chauvinism on the reservation is alive and well.

We had many discussions about our tribal constitution, and I realized that not everyone understood it. In Indian country, we all know how important civil rights are, but we're not quite sure where they come from. As important as it is, we all need more information about the constitution.

In 1916, even prior to the Indian Reorganization Act, Rosebud had a constitution and bylaws. It was obviously written by the Bureau of Indian Affairs in an attempt at organized government. The communities were organized by day schools and each had one council member as a representative. A president and vice president were chosen from among the council members, but they had no duties except to chair the meetings.

Women were not allowed to be on the council and couldn't even vote, which is not surprising since white women were not allowed to vote until 1920.

In 1934, when we accepted the Indian Reorganization Act, the federal government provided a prewritten constitution for all tribes. It was supposedly patterned after the US Constitution, but in the attempt to make it simple they left us with many problems.

The first constitution gave us a tribal council without any checks or balances. The chairman was still just that—a member of council elected to chair the meetings without the power to make decisions. The tribal judge was hired and fired by the council and was therefore subject to the influence of the council. All laws and regulations were approved or disapproved by the BIA. The people had little or nothing to say about the government.

In 1966, a constitutional amendment separated the executive branch from the legislative. From then on, the president would be elected at large. He would no longer be just the chairman of the council and would have his own authority. It would take another fifty years to make any further structural changes in our tribal government.

The Lakota Women for Change decided that it would take constitutional reform to improve our government. We had had so many complaints and suggestions from people that we knew we had to do something to give them a voice. Fortunately, Rosebud's constitution provides a process to call for a constitutional convention. It would be the perfect forum to allow all of the people to have input into the tribal government. I had day dreams of the people knowing and understanding what the tribe needed.

We would have to get the signatures of a specified number of tribal members. It wasn't going to be easy, but we decided to do it. As we set out to gather signatures, it was clear that this was going to be a monumental job. We gathered every week to count signatures and encourage everyone to keep working. We brought food and told jokes about our adventures along the way. It gave us the glue to go on with our quest.

When we finally turned in our petition, we were certain that we had more than enough valid signatures. We savored our success and talked about how we would participate in the upcoming convention. We were very disappointed when we were told that we had failed. Too many of the people who had signed the petition were not registered voters. Despite the fact the petition carriers had always asked, many people had moved to another community and failed to reregister or had simply been reluctant to admit that they weren't registered. After a few months, we decided we couldn't give up and we were ready to try again. We put on our walking shoes and began again.

We always went out in the evenings and on weekends to be sure that someone would be at home. At times it was harrowing to be in a strange place after dark. Many of the houses we visited had very little lighting. As we approached the house, we would find ourselves walking up an unpaved path that might be strewn with rocks, toys, or other obstacles. And then there were the dogs. It seemed that every house had at least one dog. Some barked ferociously, and we would sit in the car and wait for someone to come out to find out why the dogs were barking. Sometimes they were obviously mean and sometimes they just barked to announce our arrival. Others lay in the dirt, uncaring and looking up at us with soulful eyes.

Tribal housing generally has metal or concrete preconstructed stairs. Very few of them had stair rails. There were times when I had to ask someone else to climb the stairs and knock on the door because I was afraid of falling.

We traveled to the outlying communities and I met many people that I wouldn't have known otherwise. It was actually a wonderful experience. Generally, when we asked anyone to sign our petition, we had to explain what a constitutional convention would mean.

We will never forget the old man who, upon being asked to sign, replied, "I can't sign. I'm a Christian."

It was great to have the opportunity to educate people about our tribal government. I was excited at the prospect of having the convention for further education.

Along the way, I was reminded of my *Iyeska* status. Most of the women in the group were mixed-bloods. Some could speak Lakota, but most could not. We did have a few full-bloods. It didn't matter to the group, but it made a difference to some people in the communities. We ran into people who didn't like or trust *Iyeskapi* and were suspicious of any talk about constitutions. They knew that our young people seldom speak our language, but they did expect someone of my age and background to speak it. I was embarrassed to have to admit I didn't.

Once again we counted our signatures and turned in our petition, secure in the knowledge that we had more than enough signatures because we had checked the voter registration rolls to be sure. But, it wasn't to be. This time we were told we had failed because too many people had not voted in the last election and weren't eligible to sign the petition. We were crushed.

We wallowed in our failure for a while and then a miracle happened. The miracle came in the person of the chairman of the election board. She told us that it would be okay for us to gather signatures at the polls during the election. There would be specific rules, and we would not be allowed to talk about the election itself or to sit anywhere near where people were casting their ballots. We jumped at the chance.

Election Day dawned windy and cold. As the volunteers gathered, we realized that we were few in number. We had hoped to have at least two people for every polling place. We only had enough people to cover the largest communities. Undeterred, the six of us set out to carry out our mission. It was rough going in the wind and cold. Our hands and feet suffered the most.

At one point, I went to Rosebud to relieve Ollie Pretty Bird, who was ninety-four years old at the time, and she said, "No, I can do this."

Such was the dedication of our members. It was a triumphant day when we were told that we had met the criteria to have our petition validated. It had taken us three years to complete the task, and we knew it was just the beginning.

The next step was that within thirty days the tribal council was required to appoint a seven-man task force to organize the constitutional convention. The general population was allowed to apply for a position on the task force. Needless to say, I immediately put in my application. I was really disappointed when I wasn't chosen for the task force, believing that my legal skills would be an asset. Instead, we heard through the moccasin telegraph that councilmen were saying that no one in our group would be allowed to be on the task force. I swallowed my disappointment and told myself that it was okay because I would be able to contribute in some way in drafting the amendments to come.

I had the idea in my mind that the constitutional convention would be just like any other convention. I thought that there would be a gathering of the people to brainstorm what sort of changes were needed in the constitution. I assumed there would be some assistance in the actual drafting of the amendments. I was wrong.

In February 2004, the task force announced that the constitutional convention would begin by allowing tribal members to present oral and written amendments. The oral testimony would be recorded and had to be accompanied by a written copy. It was my chance to participate and I presented six proposed amendments. Twenty-three people presented various amendments over several days. In total, 182 amendments were proposed. It was an overwhelming number and would prove to be an enormous job for the task force.

From the very beginning, problems arose as the members of the task force became embroiled in internal conflict. They couldn't agree on the method to use to evaluate the amendments. Actually, there was a healthy diversity of cultural backgrounds in the membership of the task force. There were several Lakota speakers who would, I assumed, make sure that the amendments chosen would conform to Lakota culture. Since the meetings of the task force were confidential (I don't know why), I have no way of knowing what actually happened. I do know that toward the end of their deliberations, three of them resigned and were never replaced. Eventually, the tribal council got tired of giving them money and told them to finish it up. The rumors were that they had to hurry through the remaining amendments and didn't give enough consideration to all of them.

Once the task force had chosen the twenty-seven amendments that would go on the ballot, they were forwarded to the BIA, who then forwarded them to the solicitor's office. The solicitor is the attorney for the BIA, who then responded by telling the task force that there were corrections that should be made to some of the amendments. The members of the task force wanted to simply make the changes. I was concerned that once they started making changes, it was possible that they could change the meaning of the amendments. In law, one simple word—an "and," "or," "may," or "will"—can change the meaning, and it was clear that the task force wasn't getting legal advice. We, the Lakota Women for Change, were adamant that the people who wrote the amendments should be allowed to have a say in any changes. We offered, at our own expense, to bring in the amendment writers to approve any changes that might be made. Some of the members of the task force became angry.

One of them stood up, brushed his hands together, and said, "We wash our hands of this."

We were unable to move forward because, at this point, the names and addresses of the amendment proposers were confidential.

Eventually, the amendments were sent back to the BIA along with the required resolution from the tribal council. Before long, the BIA began the process of having a secretarial election.

A secretarial election is an election called by the US Secretary of the Interior and is a complicated process. The BIA is required to send registration forms to all tribal members, whether they live on the reservation or not. Once the registration is finished, they must mail out all the ballots. Many people failed to return their registration forms, and many more failed to mail in their ballots. As a result, the constitutional amendments were chosen by very few people.

There were several proposed amendments that included a proposal to change the name of our tribe from Rosebud Sioux to *Sicangu Oyate*. Unfortunately, most people who live off the reservation had not been exposed to the original name. They, along with others who wanted to maintain the status quo, rejected the change. I felt badly because, to me, it's an indication of how difficult it's going to be to move forward and it's sad to realize that the government could change our name and we'd accept it without question.

In the aftermath of the turmoil and confusion of the convention and election, people blamed the Lakota Women for Change for all the failures. They thought we had drafted the poorly written amendments and blamed us for the malfunctions of the convention and the election. We were viewed to have so much power that it was assumed we must surely be responsible. It is, I believe, a statement that change can be wrought by just a few people.

There were some errors in the new constitution that will need to be fixed with new amendments. I was pleased with some of the results of the election because we had managed to change some important aspects of the constitution and the tribal government.

I believe this was a truly historical moment in our history. First of all, we achieved a true separation of powers when the people voted to implement the amendment I wrote declaring the court free from the interference and control of the tribal council.

A stable court system is vitally important to our nation's economic growth. Separation of powers means that everyone, including nontribal members, knows that their contracts on the reservation will not be subject to political influence. The ability to trust our court could result in more businesses being willing to come to the reservation. It also means that we are closer to providing real justice for our people. As a family law practitioner, I can't tell you how many times I experienced a custody matter that was decided by a judge who was influenced by being threatened with his job. I was thrilled when the constitutional amendment was passed.

Tribal people have often complained that the federal government is involved in too many of our criminal cases. In Indian country, when a serious crime is committed and an Indian is involved, the case will be handled by the federal government. We want our tribal courts to be able to handle serious cases and to sentence them to tribal jails. Justice for our people is an important facet of our sovereignty.

Until recently, federal law also prevented tribes from sentencing anyone to more than one year in jail, which meant we could only handle minor violations of the law. In 2010, Congress passed the Tribal Law and Order Act of 2010, which allows tribal courts to give appropriate sentences for some serious crimes.[1] Tribal courts gained a little more authority.

Then, in 2013, Congress passed the Violence Against Women Act (VAWA) Reauthorization Act of 2013, which amended the Indian Civil Rights Act of 1968 to give tribes jurisdiction over non-Indians who commit acts of domestic violence on reservations.[2,3] Prior to VAWA, tribes had *no* jurisdiction over non-Indians who committed crimes on the reservation. It has long been a source of frustration for law enforcement and tribal courts. I remember one occasion when a white man decided to harass an Indian family by driving his car into their yard and destroying their porch. He repeated his actions twice, and tribal police were unable to arrest him for lack of jurisdiction. That kind of situation still exists, but we may soon be able to at least protect women in violent relationships.

There are, however, conditions that must be met before a tribe can assert such jurisdiction. Those conditions include providing licensed attorneys to act as judges and public defenders. The other major requirement is that we provide adequate jail facilities. We are moving forward in our ability to provide justice for our people, and I hope that one day the federal government will trust us enough to give us full responsibility for our own people.

Improving the court system was only one of the reforms brought about by the constitutional convention. The people voted to demand excellence in our leaders by requiring that candidates for tribal office be free of a criminal record.

The other constitutional amendment that makes me proud is the one that gives the people a way to recall tribal officials without going through the tribal council. It's in the hands of the people! That same amendment would allow the people to have input into the laws of the tribe by drafting or abolishing laws through the petition process.

It took fifty years to make the first substantial changes in our constitution and another fifty years to make more changes. I hope it won't take another fifty years to continue to improve our law. It should be an ongoing process to keep us abreast of the needs of the tribe.

Of course, not everyone is happy with the new amendments. We're still talking about the ones we don't like. What makes me happy is that we all know we have the power to change it. There is still much work to be done, and I'm happy to have had the opportunity to participate in the growth of our nation.

Watching the national and international news has caused me to compare the Lakota nations to the fledgling democratic governments of Iraq and Afghanistan. They are tribal people like us, and their struggles to move into the twenty-first century and a global economy are the same as ours. I hope the US government has learned from us that they must allow the people to choose what form their government will take. We are still struggling, after seventy-six years, to implement and understand our Constitution and our government.

Many people long for what is called "traditional government." They talk about a "treaty" government, and yet, the treaties make no mention of a specific form of government. The treaties are valuable because they told the world exactly what the federal government was giving us in exchange for the land we were forced to give up. There was no intent, in the treaties, to tell us what kind of government we should have. That came later, in 1934, when a "vote" was taken to decide whether or not we would have a constitutional government. We can't look to the treaties for direction about our form of government. We have to decide again what we need, considering where we are today and where we want to go.

We always turn to our history for advice and drawing on that history, if we had a traditional government, I assume that we would have a chief and some form of tribal council. Chiefs and other leaders were chosen, not by popularity, but because they had earned standing in the community. They were respected for their bravery and leadership skills. The people put their lives and their trust in them because they had proven themselves to be men of honor. The rules they lived by were simple, and the consequences for violation of the rules were immediate and harsh. People died if leaders were dishonorable or selfish.

If we could turn back the clock and form a traditional government, how could we choose a chief? I don't know a single person, man or woman, who I would trust with a chief's authority and power. The old chiefs didn't have a million-dollar budget or thousands of people to care for.

Today's tribal politician uses mainstream politics as a role model. On any given day you can see them whispering among themselves to decide how they will vote on a particular matter.

You can be sure they're saying, "I'll vote your way on this if you vote my way next time."

We are losing our identity as a tribal people. We don't realize that if we do what is right for the tribe, eventually it will benefit each of us individually. Some people seek election, not to make things better for the tribe, but to make things better for themselves, their families, and friends. Their real intent quickly becomes obvious as they focus on the personal benefits. Bravery, generosity, and humility seem to have flown out the window.

The world, even our little "rez" world, is not as simple as it was seventy-six years ago. We are part of the global economy and dependent on the federal government. Our own government is responsible for millions of dollars. At the same time, too many of our people live in poverty. Jobs are hard to find, and housing is at a premium. Every new council person and officer has at his or her fingertips more money and opportunity than they have had in all their lives and the possibility exists that they will never have it again. The temptations for abuse are too strong for most people. No traditional chief ever had the responsibility of so much money and power. These days, it would be unfair to expect anyone to accept such responsibility without some boundaries and rules to guide him or her.

In these modern times, rules are necessary to protect the people and the officeholders. Since the beginning of the war in Iraq and Afghanistan, we have heard political experts talking about "the rule of law." They talk about the rule of law because up to now, it has been lacking in both countries. All of the unrest in Egypt and other countries in the Mideast has been caused by people yearning for the rule of law. These people have been ruled by one single authoritarian person for many years. A chief, perhaps? They had little or nothing to say about the way their countries were run. They were getting no benefit from the money collected by their governments. They want democracy, not because they expect automatic benefits, but because they want equal opportunity to get those benefits.

Whether or not we've been aware of it, we have been operating under the rule of law since 1916. When we adopted a constitution, we agreed that we would obey it and all other laws that were put in place. We forget that democracy and the rule of law require that every person is treated the same. On the reservation, the instances in which preference is given to friends and relatives are overwhelming. Whether it's housing, utility assistance, or jobs, your rights are often ignored when stacked against the friends and relatives of those in charge. It's not right, it's not fair, and it would not have happened in a traditional society. It also indicates that we may no longer be suited to be a tribal society where everyone was treated equally.

All the tribal councils of Indian nations need to understand that it's their job to protect all the people, and the only way to do that is to abide by the law and the rules, beginning with the tribal constitution.

My hope for the future is that we will all be able to forget the pain of the past—that we each will accept our individual responsibility for maintaining the language and the culture and, most of all, we will remember our roots and show respect to one another, full-blood and *Iyeska* alike.

EPILOGUE: HOPE FOR THE FUTURE

When I started this book, I was simply fulfilling the wishes of my kids. Over the years, I can't tell you how many times they would say, "Mom, you have had an amazing life. You should write a book."

I've been a genealogy buff for years, and I gradually became aware that my children and grandchildren know very little about our family and even less about our Native American history. As the book came together, I realized that I couldn't tell my story without both histories.

My children are my true legacy. My daughters are such magnificent human beings. Terese now works as an accountant for a battered women's shelter, happy to be of service to those less fortunate than she. Jo and Neil are still married and raised six kids, including an adopted special needs child. They routinely use their lives to help others and have taught their children the benefits of giving. Jannie, whose first steps I missed, has lived a rich life in service to others. Teacher, lawyer, and defender of kids, she is now the director of an organization dedicated to protecting vulnerable women and children. Anita has chosen to be a nurse and practices her Christian mores on a daily basis to the benefit of others.

My *takója* (grandchildren) and great-grandchildren are a diverse lot. Their hair color varies from black to (shocking to me) blonde. Two of them have blue eyes, which I never anticipated in my wildest dreams. Even so, I'm proud of our United Nations family. The young people never have to worry about who they bring into the family. We welcome them all.

I look at my family and I realize I'm probably looking at the future of our tribe. Our hair, eye, and skin color may change, and maybe we'll all be *Iyeska*, but we will still be Lakota.

Those who long to resurrect the past, when we had a simple life, believe that educating our children to survive in the white world will cause us to lose our culture and that we will disappear. It is a groundless fear. Education is not the boogey man. What would cause us to lose our culture would be our failure to honor that culture, move forward with the rest of the world, and bring it with us.

I am an *Iyeska* and I am assimilated, but on my own terms. I choose when, where, and how I use the knowledge and skills I have learned. As long as we continue to teach our children and grandchildren the language, values, and traditions of the Lakota people, we will survive.

NOTES

FOREWORD

1. *Iyeska*—ee-ye-ska.

CHAPTER ONE: LAKOTA BEGINNINGS

1. Fort Laramie Treaty of 1851, 11 Stat. 749, Charles J. Kappler, ed., *Indian Affairs: Laws and Treaties: Fort Laramie Treaty with the Sioux, etc. 1851* (Washington, DC: GPO, 1904), 594; see http://digital.library.okstate.edu/kappler/Vol2/treaties/sio0594.htm.
2. Fort Laramie Treaty of 1868, 15 Stat. 635, Charles J. Kappler, ed., *Indian Affairs: Laws and Treaties: Fort Laramie Treaty with the Sioux, etc., 1868* (Washington, DC: GPO, 1904), 998; see http://digital.library.okstate.edu/kappler/vol2/treaties/sio0998.htm.
3. Treaty between the United States of America and the Sisseton and Wahpeton Bands of Dakota or Sioux Indians 1867, 15 Stat. 505; see https://www.loc.gov/law/help/statutes -at-large/40th-congress/c40.pdf.
4. Indian Appropriations Act, 1876, Ch. 289, 19 Stat 192; see http://www.loc.gov/law /help/statutes-at-large/44th-congress/session-1/c44s1ch289.pdf.
5. George E. Hyde, *Spotted Tail's Folk: A History of the Brulé Sioux* (Norman: University of Oklahoma Press, 1961), 146.
6. Hyde, 154.
7. Hyde, 148.
8. Hyde, 293–294.
9. Dawes Act or General Allotment Act of 1887. 25 USCA §331. All adult Lakota heads of household were granted 80 or 160 acres of land, which they were expected to farm.
10. Charles J. Kappler, ed., *Indian Affairs: Laws and Treaties: Agreement with the Sioux* (Washington, DC: GPO, 1904), 25 Stat. 888; see http://digital.library.okstate.edu /kappler/vol1/html_files/ses0328.html and http://digital.library.okstate.edu/kappler /vol1/html_files/ses0328.html#ch405.
11. Prior to the coming of Christianity, Lakota people would place their loved ones on a scaffold high above ground, dressed in their finest clothes and regalia.
12. John A. Anderson, Henry W. Hamilton, and Jean Tyrce Hamilton, *The Sioux of the Rosebud: A History in Pictures* (Norman: University of Oklahoma Press, 1971), 86.
13. Virginia Sneve, *Completing the Circle* (Lincoln: University of Nebraska Press, 1995).
14. *Canupa*—cha-new-pah.
15. *Iyeska*—ee-ye-ska.

16. There is no apparent source for this axiom. Some think it's African and others believe it's Native American; see https://networks.h-net.org/node/28765/pages/31934/proverb-it-takes-whole-village-raise-child.

CHAPTER TWO: GROWING UP ON THE FARM

1. Indian Reorganization Act, 25 USC §146 et seq.; see http//www.gpo.gov/fdays/pkg/USCODE-2011-title25/html.USCODE-2011title25-chap14-subchapV.htm.
2. *Sicangu*—see-chan-goo, *Oyate*—oh-yah-tay.
3. Roger Bromert, "Sioux Rehabilitation Colonies: Experiments in Self-Sufficiency, 1936–1942," in *South Dakota History,* compiler South Dakota Historical Society (Pierre: South Dakota Historical Society), 14:35.
4. *Iktómi*—eek-toe-me.

CHAPTER THREE: BOARDING SCHOOL

1. Gertrude C. Warner, *The Boxcar Children* (Morton Grove, IL: Albert Whitman Company, 1942).

CHAPTER FOUR: WHAT *IYESKA* MEANS

1. *wanáği*—wah-new-gee, *Yuwipi*—you-wee-pee.
2. *Uŋcí*—oon-chee.
3. *Siŋté*—seen-tay, *Gleŝká*—gleh-ska.

CHAPTER SIX: ASSIMILATION BEGINS

1. Displaced Persons Act, June 25, 1948, ch. 647, 62 Stat. 1009, 50 U.S.C. App. 1951 et seq.; see http://www.gpo.gov/fdsys/pkg/USCODE-2011-title50/html/USCODE-2011-title50-app-displaced.htm.

CHAPTER SEVEN: CALIFORNIA, HERE I COME

1. Indian Relocation Act, 70 Stat. 986; see http://www.gpo.gov/fdsys/pkg/STATUTE-70/pdf/STATUTE-70-Pg986.pdf.

CHAPTER ELEVEN: OBSTACLES

1. The National Congress of American Indians, formed in 1944, brings tribes together to lobby Congress and other entities.
2. Robert Burnette, *The Tortured Americans* (Englewood Cliffs, NJ: Prentice-Hall, 1971).
3. Robert Burnette and John Koster, *The Road to Wounded Knee* (New York: Bantam, 1974).

CHAPTER TWELVE: A PARADIGM SHIFT

1. American Indian Movement (AIM) is an advocacy group founded in 1968 to address Indian sovereignty, treaty issues, spirituality, and leadership.

    Wounded Knee, South Dakota, was the location of two separate incidents. In 1890, 150-plus members of Chief Big Foot's band were massacred by US troops. In 1973, Native Americans gathered at Wounded Knee under the leadership of the American Indian Movement to protest federal Indian policy; see http://www.history .com/topics/native-american-history/wounded-knee.

CHAPTER THIRTEEN: LAW SCHOOL

1. Indian Removal Act, 21st Cong., Sess. I, Ch. 148, 411 (1830).
2. Sun Tzu, *The Art of War*, trans. Basil Henry Liddel Hart (Oxford, England: University of Oxford Press, 1971).

    If you know others and know yourself, you will not be imperiled in a hundred battles; if you do not know others but know yourself, you will win one and lose one; if you do not know others and do not know yourself, you will be imperiled in every single battle.

CHAPTER FIFTEEN: RETURN TO THE CULTURE

1. *Inipi*—ee-nee-pee, sweat lodge ceremony.
2. *Tunkašila*—toon-ka-shee-la, grandfather.
3. *Hanbleceya*—han-blech-ya, also known as vision quest.

CHAPTER SIXTEEN: LIVING THE DREAM

1. Indian Child Welfare Act, 25 USCA §1901 et seq.; http://www.ssa.gov/OP_Home /comp2/F095-608.html.
2. John Ross, Principal Chief of the Cherokee nation.

CHAPTER EIGHTEEN: THE WORK GOES ON

1. Tribal Law and Order Act of 2010. PL 111-211; http://www.justice.gov/tribal/tribal-law -and-order-act.
2. Violence Against Women Act Reauthorization of 2013; http://www.gpo.gov/fdsys/pkg /BILLS-113s47enr/pdf/BILLS-113s47enr.pdf.
3. Indian Civil Rights Act of 1968, 25 USCA §1301 et seq. Violence Against Women Act of 2000, PL 106-386.